IEE CONTROL ENGINEERING SERIES 38

Series Editors: Prof. D. P. Atherton
                Dr K. Warwick

PARALLEL PROCESSING in CONTROL

the transputer and other architectures

Other volumes in this series

PARALLEL PROCESSING in CONTROL

the transputer and other architectures

Edited by:
P. J. Fleming

Peter Peregrinus Ltd. on behalf of the Institution of Electrical Engineers

Published by: Peter Peregrinus Ltd., London, United Kingdom

© 1988 Peter Peregrinus Ltd.

British Library Cataloguing in Publication Data

Parallel processing in control—the
    transputer and other architectures.
    —(IEE computing series; 38).
    1. Computer systems. Parallel-processor systems
    I.   Title   II. Series
    004'.35

ISBN 0 86341 136 3

Printed in England by Short Run Press Ltd., Exeter

Preface

Modern digital control systems typically perform real-time control and identification functions together with a number of other activities related to event logging, checking, data base management and input/output handling. These operations, in general, must be performed within a certain sample time. Hitherto, the suitability of general- purpose mini- and microcomputers for this task has been widely accepted. However, as control requirements grow, these conventional single-processor systems are unable to satisfy the demands for increased speed, greater complexity, improved dynamic range and accuracy, lower cost and greater flexibility.

Different application areas present their own individual problems. For example, in motor control, short sampling time requirements can place exacting constraints on the execution time of a control algorithm. In other application areas controller complexity increases with, for example, the number of interacting loops (e.g. robotics) or the number of sensors (e.g. vision systems). Safety- critical applications, such as aerospace and nuclear systems, present important problems associated with reliability and fault-tolerant issues. Further, the implementation of modern control algorithms founded on state-space principles, such as full state feedback controllers and Kalman filters, tends to place a considerable burden on the computer system

Accepting these new implementation requirements, control engineers have sought alternative hardware solutions, albeit possibly suffering associated increased hardware and software development costs. In the latter half of the 1970's multiprocessor systems were implemented to satisfy the new demands. Subsequently, control engineers have experimented with signal processing chips and custom designs. Special-purpose digital control computers have also been proposed. Some harness array processing power to exploit the matrix-vector operations arising from certain algorithms, while others address features such as the special input-output requirements of controllers and the separation of discrete and continuous functions.

While spectacular progress in VLSI technology has been realised over the last 15 years to increase component density, less dramatic improvements in clock speed have been forthcoming. These realities suggest that control engineers might profitably investigate parallel processing solutions for the accommodation of their increasingly demanding requirements. This interest has been further stimulated by the availability of the Inmos Transputer which provides a flexible element for the support of parallel processing for real-time applications.

The purpose of this book is twofold:-

i)   to provide an introduction to parallel processing hardware and software for control engineers, and

ii)   to review some current research and development arising from the implementation of the Transputer and alternative parallel processing architectures.

The book is arranged in four Sections :-

> **Introduction**
> **Occam and the Transputer**
> **Transputer Applications**
> **Alternative Architectures**

and reflects the special interest of the control engineering community in the Inmos Transputer and its associated parallel programming language, Occam.

The **Introduction** Section provides a general overview of parallel processing systems in a control engineering context covering both hardware and software topics. **Occam and the Transputer** specifically deals with the model of parallelism implemented on the Transputer. An introduction to the parallel programming language, Occam, is reinforced through control engineering examples and consideration of real-time issues. The architecture of the Transputer is described. **Transputer Applications** describes solutions and difficulties associated with applications in the field of motor control, flight control, robotics, and identification. An important contribution deals with the design of fault-tolerant concurrent software. **Alternative Architectures** investigates a multiprocessor solution developed in the aerospace industry, the application of systolic arrays and a new architecture for real-time control applications based on a cellular automata approach.

It is expected that the readership will have a control engineering background and an appreciation of digital controller computing requirements. The text is intended for practicing engineers, teachers, graduate and final-year undergraduate students with an interest in control engineering applications and new technological developments in parallel processing.

Acknowledgements

The book arises out of a highly successful IEE Workshop on "Parallel Processing in Control - the Transputer and other architectures" held at University College of North Wales, Bangor in September, 1987.

I would like to thank the contributors to this text for their cooperation which greatly eased the editing task. In addition, I express my thanks to Dr. D.I. Jones and Dr. S. Jones (Workshop Committee members); P. Entwistle, F. Garcia Nocetti, D.L.

Lawrie and H.A. Thompson (UCNW research workers); Mrs. G. Park and Miss S. Griffiths (for their immense help in preparation of the final version of the manuscript); Miss L. Richardson (IEE); Prof. K. Warwick (Series Editor); and J. St. Aubyn (Peter Peregrinus).

April,1988   Peter Fleming

Contents

List of contributors

S.R. Jones
School of Electronic Engineering Science
University College of North Wales

J.A. Mariani
Department of Computing Science
University of Lancaster

P.J. Fleming
School of Electronic Engineering Science
University College of North Wales

D.I. Jones
School of Electronic Engineering Science
University College of North Wales

D. May & R. Shepherd
INMOS Limited

D.J. Holding & G.F. Carpenter
Electrical & Electronic
Engineering & Applied Physics
Aston University

G. Asher & M. Sumner
Department of Electrical Engineering
University of Nottingham

D.A. Linkens & S.B. Hasnain
Department of Control Engineering
University of Sheffield

D.P.M. Wills
British Aerospace plc
Brough

G.W. Irwin & F.M.F. Gaston
Department of Electrical &
Electronic Engineering
Queens University, Belfast

Introduction

This Section provides a general overview of hardware and software issues in parallel processing systems. Despite the fact that parallel processing can be an inefficient means of speeding up computations, it is clearly shown that technological factors strongly support its application. A range of hardware architectures is described and attention is drawn to such factors as programmability, processing element functionality and inter-processor communications. The Transputer architecture is set in context as an element to be used for the construction of MIMD (Multiple-Instruction Multiple-Data) parallel processor arrays.

To support parallel processing hardware a variety of software architectures for managing concurrency is introduced. It is shown how the special requirements of parallel systems, such as synchronisation and shared variables, have been met by different languages. The discussion extends from the earliest forms of primitives for specifying parallel processes to the identification of three types of parallel programming languages: Procedure Oriented, Message Oriented and Operation Oriented. The description of Occam, which is a message-oriented language, is developed further in the next Section.

Chapter 1

Parallel processing computer architectures

Dr. Simon Jones

1.1 INTRODUCTION

Parallel processing can be defined as a technique for increasing the computation speed for a task, by dividing the algorithm into several sub-tasks and allocating multiple processors to execute multiple sub-tasks simultaneously. The objective here is to supply a concise overview of parallel processing computer architectures to provide a wider perspective within which the topics addressed in later Chapters can be better appreciated.

1.2 COMPUTATIONAL PARALLELISM

For specific problems within specific applications areas, it is possible by targeting the architecture closely to the particular problem, to improve performance almost linearly with the increase in the number of processor elements (PEs). This is 'theoretical' parallelism as it represents the maximum speed-up that can be achieved by using multiple processors. However, it is widely accepted that for general purpose applications, computational power does not increase linearly with the number of processor elements (PEs). Rather, since a proportion of the parallel computer's work-load must be executed sequentially, the 'natural' parallelism (viz. the potential for simultaneous execution of independent processes) reduces the utilisation of the 'N' processors to $O(N/\log_2 N)$.

This is the ideal case. However, since the particular structure of the parallel processing computer may not exactly match the 'natural' parallelism (eg. a 2-D array of processors attempting to solve a 3-D problem such as weather forecasting), a further reduction in processor utilisation occurs, reducing the applied parallelism to $O(\log_2 N)$.

This difference between theoretical, natural and applied parallel processing power is shown in Fig.1.1. These characteristic curves leave 3 main options available for parallel processor system designers, namely

(a) Optimise the architecture for a particular problem, with an inherent large degree of parallelism to match, and hence track the 100% PE 'theoretical' curve.

(b) Use a few very powerful processors (medium-grain parallelism) to stay close to the origin of the graph and hence use each PE efficiently.

(c) Use many small and cheap processors (fine-grain parallelism) to reduce the cost of each processor and hence to be able to increase the number of PEs cost-effectively.

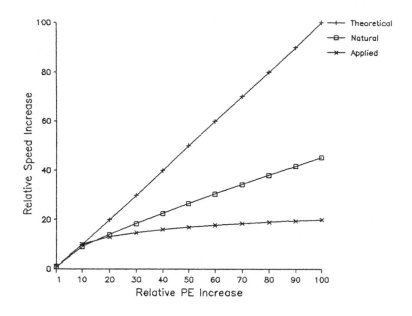

Fig.1.1 Theoretical, natural and applied parallelism.

Options 2 and 3 can be improved by making the architectural organisation flexible and programmable to more closely match the parallelism in the problem and hence get closer to the natural parallelism curve.

One important point to note from Fig.1.1 is that apart from specific problems, parallel processing appears to be a very inefficient way of speeding up computations. Indeed, a 10% speed-up in clock rates is a far more effective way of improving performance than a similar increase in the number of processors. The refutal of this argument lies in the technological characteristics of VLSI circuitry.

A characteristic of VLSI is that it enormously reduces the cost of implementing electronic systems (eg. a mainframe processor of the early 1970's using SSI technology has the same performance as the personal computer based on VLSI technology used to type these Chapters), yet the personal computer costs some 500-fold less than the mainframe. However, VLSI technology (using slow RC lines for transmission of signals) has not increased the raw clock speed of the system by anywhere near this proportion (Fig.1.2). Consequently VLSI provides ultra-cheap but relatively slow hardware. It is this economic/technological issue that is driving computer systems engineers away from the increase in clock speed and towards the application of parallelism for realising the next generation of high-performance computer systems. By providing ultra-low PE costs through VLSI technology, one can use hundreds or even thousands of PEs in parallel to cost-effectively improve computational performance.

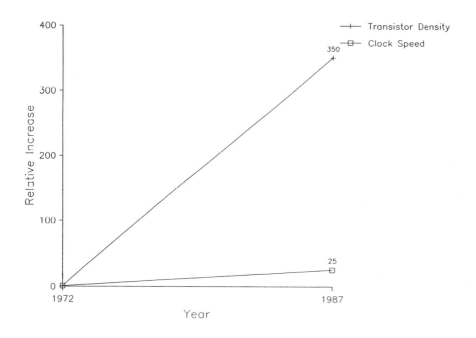

Fig.1.2 Clock speed vs Transistor packing density.

Perhaps an important point often lost in the noise, is that all the parallel processing architectures proposed could be built in virtually any technology. However, as a significant number of processors may be needed to gain large increases in performance, these architectures only become cost-effective if the cost per PE is very low while, simultaneously, gains in raw clock speed are found to be increasingly expensive.

1.3 FIXED-FUNCTION PARALLEL ARCHITECTURES

1.3.1 Pipelines

The earliest parallel architectures were fixed-function and usually based on a linear pipeline. This approach arose from the observations of computer systems engineers that the hardware of a sequential computer system was being used relatively inefficiently. Indeed, on average only about 10% of the circuitry in an non-optimised digital computer is active at any one time. The idea behind this approach is to split up the function into a number of sub-functions and for each element to receive data from its predecessor, process it and immediately pass it on to its successor (Fig.1.3). Thus all components in the pipeline can be active simultaneously. Furthermore, as each element in the pipe is small and simple, higher clock speeds can be supported. The pipe elements are usually split up into units with equal throughput delay to further enhance clock speed. The cost of the speed improvements in the pipeline is paid in the increase in the delay for one data item to be processed.

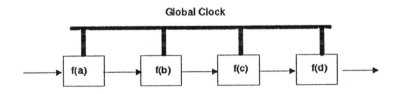

Fig.1.3 Pipeline structure.

1.3.2 Systolic Arrays

A systolic array (Fig.1.4) comprises a set of identical small processor elements regularly connected (eg. linear, array or hexagonal). Elements receive data from neighbours, process them and pass them on to their neighbours. Data may be flowing in many directions simultaneously (eg. when multiplying matrices, one matrix may be passed left to right and the other from top to bottom).

Systolic arrays with their simple structure yet high computation rates are extremely promising structures for VLSI and by targeting their function to a common problem, a wide range of applications can be supported. Indeed, GEC- Marconi currently sell a correlator chip based on a systolic array architecture [1]. Programmable systolic array chips have also been proposed (eg [2]).

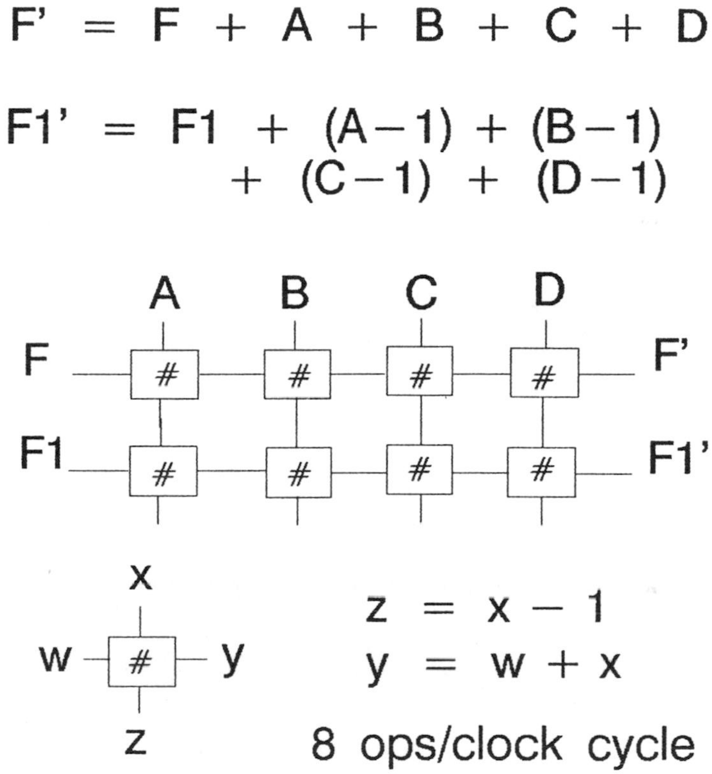

$$F' = F + A + B + C + D$$

$$F1' = F1 + (A-1) + (B-1)$$
$$+ (C-1) + (D-1)$$

$$z = x - 1$$
$$y = w + x$$

8 ops/clock cycle

Fig.1.4 Systolic array example

The disadvantage of systolic architectures is that their fixed-function allied to their neighbour connectivity and hence long throughput delay intrinsically restricts their application areas.

1.4 PROGRAMMABLE FUNCTION ARCHITECTURES

1.4.1 Fine-grain Architectures

These architectures are sometimes known as array processors (as they are usually arranged in a 2-D structure) or bit-serial processor arrays (as each PE is a simple 1-bit ALU plus memory) or SIMD (Single Instruction, Multiple Data) arrays.

As shown in Fig.1.5, an array processor comprises an interconnected set of processors with a common instruction and data busses together with an external program store. Such array processors are flexible architectures for the support and manipulation of a wide range of scalar-vector and vector-vector problems. Array processors have a long history, traceable back to the ILLIAC IV computer in the early 1960's [3] through the British DAP machine [4] up to the ESPRIT array processor [5]. Furthermore, a VLSI component for the construction of such arrays is commercially available through NCR - the GAPP chip [6], which incorporates 72 PEs on a single 84-pad VLSI chip.

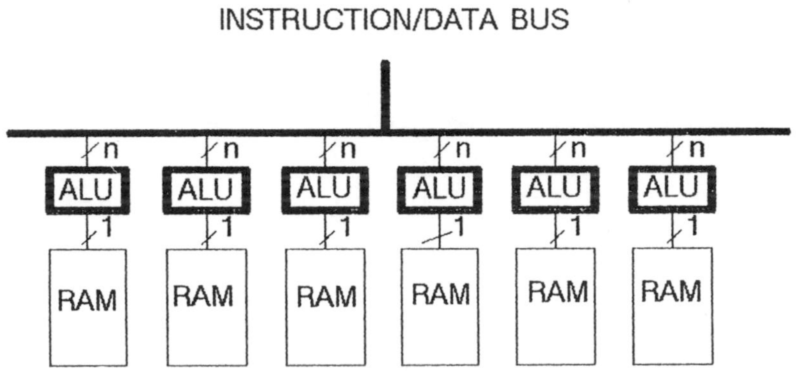

INSTRUCTION/DATA BUS

Fig.1.5. Fine-grain array processor structure.

Array processors are well suited to the commonly found number-crunching problems with large 'for' loops which can be unrolled and executed in a few passes using one PE for a small number of data items. Furthermore, the programmability of the array allows data structures other than the array to be processed in parallel by software emulation. This is however achieved at the cost of lower processor utilisation.

Perhaps the major constraint of the array processor architecture is the fact that all processors have to execute the same instruction. For applications which require different algorithms to be applied to different portions of the data set the SIMD architecture is much less efficient. Indeed, when different algorithms need to be applied to each data item then the performance of the SIMD architecture is worse than that of a sequential microprocessor.

A major advantage of the SIMD architecture is that its operation fits well within the paradigm of sequential programming. Programs are still written sequentially, but the 'for' loops with operations and index counters are merely replaced with 'forall' instructions which execute the entire loop in relatively few passes. Furthermore, the single instruction stream means that the same code can be used irrespective of the number or changes in the number of processors in the array.

1.4.2 Medium-grain Architectures

The PEs of medium-grain parallel architectures are significantly more complex than those of fine-grain architectures. They possess local program store (Fig.1.6) and are usually bit-parallel rather than bit-serial devices. Currently a range of medium-grain architectures based on a range of topologies are well developed (eg. COSMIC cube [7] or the IBM RP3 [8]), however within a UK context, the INMOS Transputer is the best known. (It is described in more detail in Chapter 6.)

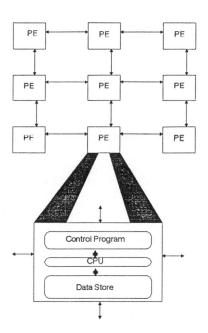

Fig.1.6 Medium-grain array structure

Strictly speaking the Transputer is a VLSI 32-bit microprocessor with on-board RAM and floating-point capability. However, the inclusion of on-silicon communications links and protocols allows it to be used as a low-cost component for the construction of medium-grain, or MIMD (Multiple-Instructions, Multiple Data) parallel processor arrays (cf. the GAPP chip for SIMD arrays).

The primary advantage of MIMD over SIMD is that different algorithms can be performed simultaneously over the data set. The price paid for this in hardware terms is the increase in PE cost (eg. the GAPP chip packs 72 PEs on a similarly sized chip and technology as the 1 PE on the Transputer). However, with the continuing advance of VLSI technology this overhead will decrease.

Perhaps the major obstacle to the success of these highly-flexible and powerful machines will be in terms of software. With sequential machines software costs tend to dominate system costs. With multi-processor arrays executing hundreds or even thousands of asynchronous communicating processes simultaneously, the software overheads of assuring correctness and reliability are multiplied enormously. In later Chapters it will be demonstrated that OCCAM, with its synchronisation primitives, is a considerable advance on conventional programming languages and a powerful tool for the description of parallel systems. Nonetheless, it still relies on the software engineer to assure semantically correct synchronisation and data passing. Perhaps for MIMD structures to be fully utilised, higher-level CAD tools will need to be generated which can identify and implement parallel processes automatically and independently of the software engineer.

1.5. CONCLUSIONS

This Chapter has reviewed the application and types of parallel processing computer architectures. It has shown that the technological characteristics of VLSI provide a strong incentive to computer systems engineers to utilise parallelism as a technique for improving the performance of future generation computer systems.

Fixed and programmable function architectures have been reviewed and their merits and demerits considered. Fine- grain (SIMD) arrays perhaps make most cost-effective use of silicon, but their restriction of single instruction streams limits the range of applications that can be supported. Medium-grain (MIMD) parallelism is more expensive in terms of silicon, but the local stored program capability significantly enhances its flexibility. In any case the continued improvement in VLSI technology means that the hardware costs are likely to decrease and it is the cost of implementing reliable correct parallel asynchronous software systems that may cause the greatest limitations. Even so, the technological characteristics of VLSI allied to the increasing demand for higher performance computer systems means that parallel architectures are likely to be an increasingly common solution to the quest for speed.

REFERENCES

1.Corry, A.G. and Patel, K., 1983, 'A CMOS/SOS VLSI Correlator', Proceedings 1983 International Symposium on VLSI Technology Systems Applications, pp. 134-137.

2.Fisher, A. and Kung, H.T., 1985, 'Special-purpose VLSI Architectures: General Discussions and a Case Study', in VLSI and Modern Signal Processing, (S.Y. Kung, H.J. Whitehouse, T. Kailath Eds), Prentice Hall Information and Systems Science Series 1985.

3.Barnes, G.H., Brown, H., Kato R., Kuck, M., Slotnick, D.J. and Stokes, R.A., 1968, 'The Illiac IV Computer', Proceedings IEEE Transactions on Computers, Vol. C-17, pp. 746-757.

4.Roberts, J.B.G., Simpson, P., Merrifield, R.C. and Cross, J.F., 1984, 'Signal Processing Applications of a Distributed Array Processor', Proceedings IEE Computers and Digital techniques, No. 131, Pt E, pp.294-305.

5.Ivey, P.A., Huch, M., Glesner, M., and Midwinter, T., 1987, 'Design of a Large SIMD Array in Wafer-Scale Technology', Proceedings of the IFIP Workshop on Wafer- Scale Integration, Brunel University, 1987, Paper 2.3.

6.Dettmer, R., 1985, 'Chip Architectures for Parallel Processing', IEE Electronics and Power, March, 1985, pp. 227-231.

7.Seitz, C.L., 1985, 'The Cosmic Cube', Communications of the ACM, Vol. 28, No. 1, pp. 22-33.

8.Pfister, G.F., Brantley, W.C., George, D.A. and Harvey, S.L., Kleinfelder, W.J., McAuliffe, K.P., Melton, E.A., Norton, V.A. and Weiss, J., 1985, 'The IBM Research Parallel Processor Prototype (RP3): Introduction and Architecture', Proceedings 1985 International Conference on Parallel Processing, pp. 764-711.

Chapter 2

An introduction to parallel programming languages and software architectures

Dr. J.A. Mariani

2.1 INTRODUCTION

In this Chapter, we will review a number of software architectures that help the programmer to organise and synchronise a number of parallel processes or tasks. We shall also briefly examine two specific systems, MASCOT and CONIC.

The architectures we will examine include :

> Semaphores
> Monitors
> Remote Procedure Calls
> Ada's Rendezvous
> Object message passing

We shall consider both the situations of :

a) parallel processes running on the same machine, and

b) parallel processes running on different machines/processors; the machines will be linked either by buses (in the case of tightly coupled processors) or local area networks.

In order that parallel processes can cooperate, there has to be a flow of information between them; there has to be a communications medium. In case (a) above, there can be a shared memory area where values can be read/written. In case (b), messages will have to be formed and sent along the bus/local area network.

2.1.1 Specifying Parallel Processes

One of the earliest forms of primitives for specifying parallel processes were the **fork** and **join** primitives.

```
program P1          program P2
----                ----
   fork P2;            ----
----                ----
   join P2;            end;
----
```

Execution of P2 is initiated when the **fork** in P1 is executed; P1 and P2 then execute concurrently until either P1 reaches the **join** statement or P2 terminates. Variants of **fork** and **join** can be found in the UNIX operating system, where **fork** provides a direct mechanism for dynamic process creation.

A more structured way of giving a list of statements to be executed concurrently is the **cobegin** (or **parbegin**) statement.

cobegin S1 || S2 || --- || Sn **coend**

Occam has the equivalent in the form of the PAR statement. Notice that **cobegin** can only be used to activate a fixed number of processes, whereas **fork** can create an arbitrary number.

2.1.2 The Producer/Consumer Problem

A classic example used to illustrate the problems posed by parallel programming is the producer/consumer problem. Here we have a process (the producer) which generates a stream of data that we wish to send to another process (the consumer). As there may be fluctuations on the rate of consumption/production of data, we interpose a bounded buffer between the two processes in order to smooth out such fluctuations. The buffer is assumed to reside in a common memory area; this places us in case (a), above.

We can now define some interface routines for the two processes :

insert(x) stores a data item x in the buffer
extract(x) retrieves it
full returns the value true if the buffer is full
empty returns the value true if the buffer is empty

Our first solution might be :

```
producer : do
               produce(x);
               while full do wait;
               insert(x)
           end do

consumer : do
               while empty do wait;
               extract (x)
               consume(x)
           end do
```

At first glance, this seems quite reasonable. However, this will not work as simultaneous access to the shared buffer can occur and we therefore run the risk of corrupting the data (i.e. we could issue an **extract** and **insert** at the same time). The sections of code involved in accessing the shared resource are known as **critical sections.** We have to identify the shared resource (the buffer) and ensure mutually exclusive access to the resource. This can be done by using Dijkstra's semaphores.

2.2. SOFTWARE ARCHITECTURES

2.2.1 Semaphores [1]

A semaphore is a non-negative integer which, apart from initialisation, can only be acted upon by the semaphore operations, wait (or P) and signal (or V). The definition of these operators is as follows.

signal(s) :increase the value of the semaphore s by one

wait(s) : decrease the value of the semaphore s by 1, as soon as the result would be non-negative.

Both these operations are (and must be) indivisible. The effects can be summarised as follows :

wait(s) : when s 0 do s := s-1
signal(s) : s := s + 1;

Thus, we can enclose critical sections (those sections accessing a resource requiring mutual exclusion) with wait and signal operations on a single semaphore whose initial value is 1.

wait(mutex);
   critical section
signal(mutex);

We can also use semaphores to achieve synchronisation. For example, we do not wish the producer to attempt to add items to the buffer when it is full, nor the consumer to extract items when the buffer is empty. We attempted to deal with this problem in the model solution above. Both producer and consumer have "busy wait" loops; they wait until the buffer is not full or not empty. Busy waits are obviously unsatisfactory as they waste processor time. We can use semaphores instead to signal the appropriate conditions (i.e. buffer not full, buffer not empty).

We introduce the following three semaphores :

> buffer access
> non full
> non empty

and this gives rise to the following solution :

```
producer : do
              produce(x);
              if full then wait(non full);
              wait(buffer access);
              insert(x);
              signal(buffer access);
              signal(non empty)
              end do

consumer : do
              if empty then wait(non empty);
              wait(buffer access);
              extract(x);
              signal(buffer access);
              signal(non full);
              consume(x)
              end do
```

2.2.2 Monitors [2]

A monitor is a module which encapsulates shared data with a set of procedures that access that data. A basic rule of a monitor is that only one process at a time can call a monitor procedure within a given monitor. This gives us a high-level construct for achieving mutually exclusive access to a shared resource. In this case, we would form a monitor that contained the buffer and the four interface procedure / functions listed above; we can no longer call **extract** and **insert** at the same time.

Using monitors, then, to provide mutual exclusion we can drop the semaphore **buffer access**. This gives us the following solution :

```
producer : do
              produce(x);
              if full then wait(non full);
              insert(x);
              send (non empty)
          end do

consumer : do
              if empty then wait (non empty);
              extract (x);
              send (non full);
              consume(x)
          end do
```

Notice, however, we retain the synchronisation semaphores. Monitors share the benefits of modules in that a single monitor can be developed and tested in isolation. The signals involved in the correct operation of the monitor are also encapsulated and therefore hidden from the rest of the system. In fact, we can hide all the communication requirements within the monitor and provide the user with (in this case) two simple interface routines, (say) transmit and receive. Monitors have been implemented in Concurrent PASCAL [3] and Modula [4]; both these languages have been used in process control applications.

Monitors are centred on the protection of shared memory; in the more loosely coupled systems, there is no shared memory to protect. Communication takes place by message passing. We must look at other methods.

We move on to describe the situation on a local area network.

2.2.3. Remote Procedure Calls

In this model, we designate the two communicating processes as a client and a server. The client issues a request to the server; the server carries out the request, and sends a result/reply. The request has the following form :

operation identifier : parameters

A server may have various functions it can perform; we select this function by an identifier. The function may also require some parameters; these also have to be supplied. The response has the following form

result code : results

We can show the operation of the client server model in Fig.2.1 below.

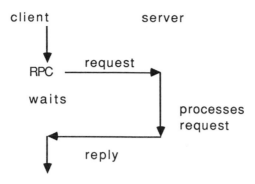

Fig.2.1 Client server model

We can provide a local procedure which acts as an interface to the communications mechanism :

result = do (server_name, selector, (parameters), (results));

The underlying software packages up the request message, sends it, and awaits the reply. Synchronisation is achieved because a message can be received only after it has been sent, which constrains the order in which these two events can occur.

The RPC is so called as it has the same semantics as a local procedure call; there should appear to be no difference between an LPC and an RPC. However, as message passing across a network is involved, the implementation of an RPC mechanism has to take into account the possibilities of request or replies going astray. For example, the client may have a fixed time it will wait for a reply before timing out and sending the request again. However, this could result in the server receiving two requests -- i.e. being asked to do the same thing twice. If the execution of the remote function has an incremental effect (i.e. increase the value of some variable by one) then after two requests it will have erroneously increased the value by two. We have two options to tackle this problem

a) only allow requests which can be repeated i.e. repeated executions of an operation must be equivalent to a single execution; such services are known as "idempotent". In general, this limits the services we can offer, or

b) implement mechanisms which insure a remote operation is executed (exactly) once; using an atomic transaction mechanism, we can arrive at exactly once or never semantics. This is important to ensure we do not leave data in a "halfway" state of a transformation.

2.2.4 The Ada Rendezvous

The technique used in Ada is akin to that of CSP (and therefore occam). A process invokes a remote operation by calling a service in a similar manner to calling a remote procedure. The name of the server as well as the service and parameters must be provided. As in the RPC, the client process is delayed until a reply is received. The operation does not take place until the server is ready to accept a call for the required service. At that time, the server accepts the call, executes the appropriate commands, and then returns the results to the client. The interchange of data occurs only when both partners are read to read/write; this establishes synchronisation. The two processes are then free to carry on with their independent operation.

This approach may be unsuitable for certain applications whereby processes cannot wait or may have to interact with others in a "random" (i.e. unpredictable) order. For example, a server can expect "simultaneous" requests from any number of clients.

Attempts to introduce indeterminacy have focussed on guarded commands. A guarded command consists of a sequence of boolean expressions (or guards) and associated actions. All the guards are evaluated simultaneously and one of those which evaluated to true is chosen nondeterministically and its associated action is executed.

In Ada, we specify a process by the keyword **task.**

We can now present the Ada rendezvous solution to the producer/consumer problem [5]:

```
task body buff is

buffer : array (0 .. maxbuf) of object;
count : integer range 0 .. bufsize := 0;
nextin, nextout : integer range 0 .. maxbuf := 0;

begin
  loop
    select
      when count < bufsize => { room in buffer }
        accept insert(ob:in object)   {accept rendezvous}
          buffer(nextin) := ob;       {input data}
        end insert                    {end rendezvous}
        nextin := ( nextin +1) mod bufsize;
        count := count + 1;           { do housekeeping }
  or                                  { next select option }
      when count > 0 =>               {data in buffer}
        accept extract (ob : out object);
          ob := buffer(nextout);      {extract data}
        end extract                   {end rendezvous}
        nextout := ( nextout +1) mod bufsize;
        count := count -1;            {do housekeeping}
    end select
  end loop
end buff
```

Notice that the complexion of the solution has changed; where we had a static buffer, we now have an active process containing the buffer.

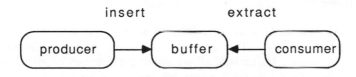

Fig.2.2 Producer, Buffer, Consumer

2.2.5 The Object Oriented approach

The use of objects emerged in several fields; the Object model [6] was suggested as a structuring aid for operating systems, the Actor model [7,8] for AI programming, and the Frame [9] for knowledge representation. Object oriented design and programming methodologies are currently very much in vogue. Objects consist of a set of data and a set of allowable operations (methods) that manipulate the data. Operations are invoked by sending the object a message that contains a selector for the required method. The message may include parameters for the operation. An object can thus be described as a logical or physical entity which is self contained and provided with a unified communication protocol.

One of the better known object oriented systems is Smalltalk [10]. However, many other programming languages now have object oriented dialects i.e. Loops (Lisp), Object Pascal etc. The C programming language has one called Objective-C [11]. This is implemented by a preprocessor that converts an Objective-C program into a C program with calls to a run time package. The main argument for a language like Objective-C is that Smalltalk is a full environment; we could not use it to develop C level systems programs. With Objective-C, however, we can have the best of both worlds (or fall between two stools, it depends on your attitude).

The message passing of Objective-C (and Smalltalk) is semantic; it really boils down to a procedure call. Both these systems are linear; there is no parallelism involved.

It would seem that since an object is a self-contained entity provided with a unified communication protocol, it can be used as a unit of concurrent programming. In the Orient84/K [12] system, objects can run concurrently with others, and a computation consists of a parallel exchange of messages.

2.2.6. Message Passing Semantics

At this point, we can consider some semantics of message passing. So far, we have discussed synchronous communication; if we send a message in the rendezvous model, we wait till the receiver can accept it. In the RPC, we wait for a reply. These involve us either in a "busy wait" which wastes processor time, or in a process suspension, waiting for a signal to wake us up. The latter involves a process manager, which must queue and schedule processes; this activity also occupies a finite time.

In some cases, we have an alternative, if we can send a message and not (immediately) await a reply. This is a "no wait send", and provides us with asynchronous messaging. Orient84/K allows either synchronous or asynchronous messaging. We would argue that this approaches maximizes parallelism.

2.2.7. Real Time Considerations

In control applications, there will be hard time constraints. The overhead of accessing protected shared memory may be too large; the overhead of messaging across a local area network is even greater!

Even on a multiprocessor machine, chances are there will be more virtual processes than processors. There is a requirement for a manager process, to swap processes in and out of memory while they are waiting for a signal to arrive. The time taken for the manager algorithms to execute must be taken into account.

We must be able to synchronise with time itself; we should have access to a system-wide real time clock. In our discussion on RPCs, we noted the idea of a "timeout". If we send a message, we cannot wait forever for a reply; we can specify how long we are willing to wait.

2.3. MODELS OF CONCURRENT PROGRAMMING LANGUAGES

In conclusion, we can identify three types of parallel programming languages: Procedure Oriented (POL), Message Oriented (MOL) and Operation Oriented (OOL) [13].

Processes in POLs interact via shared variables (or shared objects). Shared objects are subject to concurrent access; we have to have some means of ensuring mutual exclusion.

Both MOLs and OOLs are based on message passing. In MOLs, there are no shared, passive objects; an object is managed by a single **caretaker** process, which performs all operations on it. A caretaker can carry out only one operation at a time, so we can never have concurrent access. A caretaker receives a request, carries it out, and (possibly) sends a reply. CSP is an example of an MOL.

OOLs provide RPCs as the primary means of process interaction. As in an MOL, each object has a caretaker; as in a POL, operations are carried out by calling a procedure. In an OOL, the caller and the caretaker synchronise while the operation is executed. Ada is an example of an OOL.

In the three concurrent programming situations we have identified -- uniprocessors, multiprocessors and distributed systems -- we can now specify which type of language is suited to each situation. POLs are best suited to uniprocessors. It is costly to simulate shared memory where none exists, so POLs on distributed systems can be prohibitive. MOLs can be implemented with or without shared memory. OOLs can be implemented either as a POL if shared memory exists, or as a MOL with message-passing.

2.4 PARALLEL PROGRAMMING SUPPORT SYSTEMS

In this Section, we examine two specific software systems which support parallel programming.

2.4.1. MASCOT [14]

The MASCOT system (Modular Approach to Software Construction, Operation and Test) is a system with an accurate acronym; it is aimed at supporting the construction, operation and testing of systems built with software modules or processes.

The run time unit of activity -- which is the MASCOT module, the unit or thread of multi-programming -- is known as an **activity** (we would call it a process). Activities communicate via Intercommunication Data Areas (or IDAs). There are two classes of IDA; a **channel** which carries a flow of data, and a **pool** which holds a reservoir of data.

MASCOT diagrams allow us to represent a configuration of activities and IDAs. The elements of a MASCOT diagram are represented as shown in Fig.2.3.

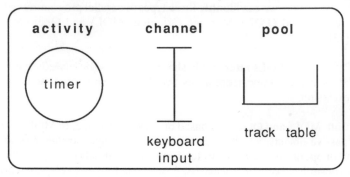

Fig.2.3 MASCOT diagram elements

A simple "producer consumer" situation can be represented as shown below in Fig.2.4.

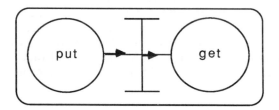

Fig.2.4 ACP representation of Producer Consumer

Such diagrams are known as Activity Channel Pool diagrams, or ACPs. We can design our software configuration in terms of MASCOT diagrams, which remain visible throughout the software life cycle.

Notice that synchronisation is a matter of accessing the IDAs. This means that we can isolate all multiprocessing problems in the routines which access the IDAs (i.e. in the form of **extract** and **insert** routines), which are called in the rest of the single activity that we can regard (and therefore write) as a single threaded mono program.

MASCOT uses a **control queue** in place of a semaphore. We can join, leave, wait or stimulate a queue. **join** and **leave** are used in the manner of Dijkstra's wait and signal to effect mutual exclusion of an IDA. **wait** and **stim** are used to provide the mechanism for synchronisation.

When a MASCOT system is running, the MASCOT kernel is in charge of scheduling activities. Moreover, it is possible to replace an activity with an alternative one while the system is running, or for the system terminal to be use in place of the removed activity. This gives us some powerful testing capabilities. Note that the diagrams we have used are from the original MASCOT; [14] has details of the most recent version, MASCOT 3.

2.4.2. CONIC [15,16]

The CONIC architecture provides an integrated approach to distributed computer control systems. CONIC modules (the unit of distribution) are interconnected by linking their **exitports** to the **entryports** of other module instances. Take, for example, the ward monitoring system example illustrated in Fig.2.5.

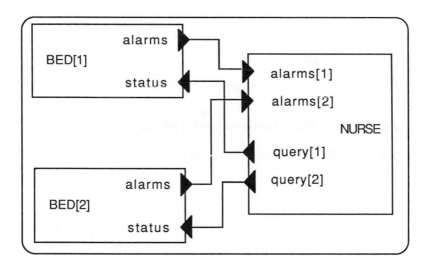

Fig.2.5 CONIC system

The CONIC programming language is based on Pascal, to which message passing primitives have been added. The message primitives provide both uni-directional asynchronous and bi-directional request-reply message transactions (i.e. remote procedure calls). We can define messages using standard Pascal type declarations.

We can use a system configuration language to use existing module types, create named instances of those types, and link **entryports** to **exitports.**

It is possible to change a configuration using a similar language i.e. if we wish to replace the NURSE by a NEWNURSE we can unlink the NURSE from the BEDS, delete NURSE, create a NEWNURSE and then link NEWNURSE to the BEDS. This activity can be performed dynamically.

ACKNOWLEDGEMENTS

I would like to thank my colleagues, John Gallagher, Andrew Scott, and Craig Wylie for their comments on earlier drafts of this Chapter.

REFERENCES

1.Dijkstra, E.W., 1968, "Cooperating sequential processes", in Programming Languages (ed. F. Genuys), Academic Press, New York.

2.Hoare, C.A.R., 1974, "Monitors : an operating system structuring concept", Communications of the ACM, Vol.17, No.10, pp. 549-557.

3.Brinch Hansen, P., 1975, "The programming language Concurrent Pascal", IEEE Transactions on Software Engineering, Vol.SE-1, No.2, pp. 199-206.

4.Wirth, N., 1977, "Modula : a language for modular multiprogramming", Software, Practice and Experience, Vol.7, pp 3-35.

5.Whiddett, R., 1986, "Distributed programs : an overview of implementations", Microprocessors and microsystems, Vol.10, No.9, pp. 475-484.

6.Jones, A.K., 1978, "The object model : a conceptual tool for structuring software", in Operating Systems -- An Advanced Course, Springer-Verlag, Heidelberg, pp. 8-16.

7.Hewitt, C., 1977, "Viewing Control Structures as Patterns of Passing Messages", Artificial Intelligence, Vol. 8, pp. 323-364.

8.Hewitt, C., and Baker, H., 1977, "Laws for Communicating Parallel Processes", Information Processing 1977, pp. 987-992.

9.Minsky, M., 1975, "A Framework for Representing Knowledge", The Psychology of Computer Vision, Winston, P. (ed), McGraw-Hill.

10.Goldberg, A., and Robson, D., 1983, Smalltalk-80 : The language and its implementation, Addison-Wesley.

11.Ledbetter, L., and Cox, B., 1985, "Software-ICs", BYTE, (June 1985), pp 307-316.

12.Tokoro, M., and Ishikawa, Y., 1986, "Concurrent Programming in Orient 84/K : An Object-Oriented Knowledge Representation Language", SIGPLAN Notices, Vol. 21, No. 10, pp. 39-48.

13.Andrews, G.R., and Schneider, F.B., 1983, "Concepts and Notations for Concurrent Programming", ACM Computing Surveys, Vol.15, No.1. pp. 3-44.

14.IEE Software Engineering Journal, Special issue on Mascot 3, Vol. 1, No. 3, May 1986.

15.Kramer, J., Magee, J., Sloman, M., and Lister, A., 1983, "CONIC : an integrated approach to distributed computer control systems", IEE Proc., Vol.130, Pt.E, No.1.

16.Kramer, J., Magee, J., and Sloman, M., 1983, "Dynamic system configuration for distributed real-time systems", pp. 31-42, in Real-Time Programming 1983, G.M. Bull, ed., Pergamon Press.

Occam and the transputer

The Occam model of parallelism is introduced. Occam is a message oriented language whose basic unit is a "process". Synchronisation is achieved by means of communication channels and, since processes cannot share variables, transmission of variables is accomplished through the use of these channels. The constructs of the language are introduced and it is demonstrated how they may be used to assemble basic architecture components.

Control engineering examples are used to demonstrate how parallelism might be exploited using Occam. A parallel version of a predictor-corrector algorithm for numerical integration involving three Occam processes is described. Next, a possible structure of Occam processes for a parallel line search in association with an optimisation method is proposed. In the third example, it is shown how a parallel description of a real-time control system might be expressed. In each example, dataflow characteristics are defined early in the design of the software which proceeds by means of structure diagrams and the development of pseudo-code.

A more detailed description of the language follows, its aim being to facilitate understanding of subsequent applications Chapters. Special consideration is given to real-time operations, priority assignment, deadlock, the use of guards and the mechanism for allocation of processes onto processors.

Finally, a target processor (and the only one to date), the Transputer, is examined. It is a RISC (Reduced Instruction Set Computer) machine with distinctive inter-processor communication facilities. The efficient implementation of its compact instruction set is outlined. The Transputer uses point-to-point serial communication links for direct communication with other Transputers. These links support the Occam model for communication over channels. Since it is feasible to allocate more than one process per processor, the organisation of both internal and external channel communication is described.

Chapter 3

Occam model of parallelism

Dr. P.J. Fleming

3.1 INTRODUCTION

3.1.1 Sequential Programming

A sequential programming language is characterised by its actions occurring in a strict, single execution sequence. The behaviour of the program depends only on the effects of the individual actions and their order. The time taken to perform the action is not of consequence.

Programming in a sequential language requires the decomposition of an algorithm into a set of operations occurring in strict order. However, the resulting order is often arbitrary. Consider, for example, the Pascal code to add two matrices:

```
begin
   for i := 1 to index do
      for j := 1 to index do
         matC[i,j]:= matA[i,j] + matB[i,j];
end;
```

Here, matC[1,1] is calculated first, followed by matC[1,2], and so on. Since no ordering is required by the algorithm, it is not essential that the calculations be performed in this order. Indeed, since each of the additions is independent of the others, they could each be executed in parallel.

3.1.2 Parallel Programming

A parallel program may consist of a number of tasks or processes which are themselves purely sequential, but which are executed concurrently and which communicate through shared variables and synchronization signals.

It is now quite common to find computer systems capable of executing several programs concurrently. A multiprocessor system consists of several central processing units (CPUs) sharing the same memory, while a parallel or distributed computer system has several (possibly many) computers each with its own CPU and memory, connected with communication links into a network. In these systems, many tasks can execute concurrently.

Even on a single processor it is often useful to design a program consisting of several tasks intended to run concurrently. In this case, the illusion of concurrent execution is created through time-sharing the various tasks on the single processor. Bearing in mind the concurrent nature of the real world, it is perhaps desirable to seek to model and control it on a computer system using a parallel programming language.

3.2 CONCURRENCY ISSUES

During the concurrent execution of several tasks, each task proceeds asynchronously with the others, that is, each task proceeds at its own speed. In order for two tasks running asynchronously to coordinate their activities, the programming language must provide a means of synchronization.

For example, one task may be handling input from an analog-to-digital converter (ADC) while a second task computes a control output level. The first task reads the input from the ADC, scales it and signals the second task that the input information is ready. The second task waits for the signal from the first task, processes the input data to generate the control output level, then signals the first task that it has completed the processing and waits again for the signal that another batch of input data is ready. The first task may be handling a second batch of input signals at the same time that the second task is processing the control level based on the first batch of input data. The signals sent between the tasks allow the tasks to synchronize their activities so that the second does not start computing the control law before the first task has finished processing its measurement data input.

Important problems involved in dealing with concurrency are the synchronization issue and the handling of shared variables between concurrent tasks. In Chapter 2 we saw that a number of mechanisms has been invented involving such devices as semaphores, monitors, remote procedure calls and so on. However, using these devices the burden of ensuring that concurrent tasks are synchronized falls on the programmer. Occam seeks to alleviate this burden.

3.3 OCCAM MODEL [1],[2]

The basic unit of occam programming is a "process" that performs a set of operations and then terminates. This concept is similar to conventional programming languages, except that, in occam, there may be more than one process executing at any given time. (Occam has arisen from work by Hoare [3] on the mathematics of communicating sequential processes.)

Occam processes are built from three primitive processes :-

assignment, input and **output.**

These primitive processes are combined to form constructs :

SEQ sequential **PAR** parallel **ALT** alternative

IF conditional **WHILE** iteration.

A construct is itself a process and may be used as a component of another construct, thereby providing the capability hierarchically to decompose complex problems.

(Compare this with conventional sequential programs, expressed with variables and assignments combined to form sequential, conditional and iterative constructs.)

Communication between processes is via point-to-point links known as "channels". Components of a parallel construct do not share access to variables. Instead, they communicate solely through channels. These channels are one-way and self-synchronizing, so that communication only takes place when both the sender and receiver processes are ready. If one process becomes ready before the other, then it will automatically wait for the other, without any explicit command from the programmer. The only responsibility left with the programmer is that of avoiding deadlock by ensuring that the second process becomes ready sometime.

3.3.1 Occam Primitives

Processes in occam are built from three "primitive" processes:

(a) The assignment statement

v := e

where the variable "v" is set to the value of the expression.

(b) The input command

c ? v

where a value is sought from a channel named "c" and will be stored in the variable named "v".

(c) The output command

c ! e

where the value of the expression named "e" is output to the channel.

When an output command is encountered in a process, the process is halted until another process has executed the corresponding input command. In this way, communication cannot proceed until both processes are ready to perform the I/O transfer.

3.3.2 SEQ and PAR Constructions

Several primitive processes can be combined into a larger process by specifying that they should be performed in sequence or in parallel.

SEQ construct:

signifies that the statements inside the process are to be executed sequentially.

A simple example of an occam program is the following process where a measurement signal is input from an ADC, scaled and the result output to a DAC:

```
SEQ
  ADC?  meas.signal
  scaled.signal := meas.signal * scale.factor
  DAC! scaled.signal
```

(Throughout this Chapter, type declarations are omitted from the occam coding examples.)

Indentation is used to indicate program structure. In this example, it denotes that the three lines following SEQ are components of that process. The program consists of setting meas.signal to the value from channel ADC, scaling it and outputting scaled.signal to the channel DAC. A SEQ process therefore works just like a program in a conventional programming language. It should be noted, though, that when two or more processes are to run in sequence, then the sequential mode, SEQ, must be explicitly requested.

Fig.3.1 SEQ construct example

The direct relationship between the code and the illustration, Fig.3.1, is important, as a representation of the processes and their connections is a good design starting point.

PAR construct:

indicates that the following processes are to be executed independently of each other. In the following example, processes 1 and 2 can be initiated in parallel:

```
PAR
    ... process 1
    ... process 2
```

The convention of ... will be used to prefix parts of a program, whose internal details are not relevant to the example.

The use of indentation denotes that the corresponding statements are part of the same process, i.e., in the above example, process 1 and process 2 are component processes of the governing PAR process. The operation of parallel processes is represented in Fig.3.2, where each of the individual processes may be assumed to be similar to the previous SEQ example.

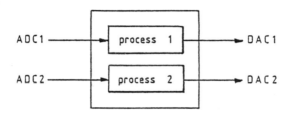

Fig.3.2 PAR construct example

It would improve comprehension of this construction if we used the following format:

```
PAR
    ... process 1                              ... process 2
```

which visually demonstrates concurrent execution of the two processes. However, it will be appreciated that this format is not viable when one considers the width of VDU screens and the possible occurrence of more than two or three parallel processes in a PAR. It is therefore important to bear in mind that the written order of the component in a PAR is irrelevant. (The written order is relevant in the prioritised version of the PAR construct; this is discussed in Chapter 5).

Parallel processes, therefore, run at the same time and, in general, they run asynchronously, i.e. at their own pace. Synchronisation is only necessary when processes need to communicate over a channel.

3.3.3 Shared variables

Communication between the component processes of a PAR must only be carried out over channels. Occam does not permit transmission of values between parallel processes by using a shared variable. For example, the following code is ILLEGAL in its use of the variable "m":

```
PAR
  SEQ
    m := 0
    ... more processes
  SEQ
    m := m+1
    ... more processes
```

Instead, transmission of the value of variable "n" is accomplished through the use of a channel:

```
PAR
  SEQ
    m := 0
    chan! m+1
    ... more processes
  SEQ
    chan? n
    ... more processes
```

This will be readily appreciated when one considers what would happen if transmission of values via shared variables were allowed. Since processes run asynchronously, if one process read from a variable whose value is altered in another parallel process - what value will be read? It depends on whether the value has been altered by the time the first process reads the variable.

3.3.4 ALT construct

The ALT construct is used in cases where a subset of the input channels may be used to initiate computations within a process. ALT operates a "first-wins" procedure, executing only the process associated with the first input to become ready.

In the following example, if input.channel2 was the first to produce an input, then only process 2 would be executed.

```
ALT
  input.channel1? x
    ... process 1
  input.channel2? x
    ... process 2
  input.channel3? x
    ... process 3
```

Each component of an ALT construct begins with a test condition. For example, input.channel1? x tests whether input.channel1 is ready. This test condition or "guard" may be a Boolean expression, viz.:

$$(y = 0) \text{ \& input.channel1? } x$$

If more than one of the guards is TRUE, then any one, and only one, of the processes governed by a TRUE guard may be performed.

Output guards are a very convenient programming tool. However, the provision of output guards would greatly complicate the communications protocol; they are, therefore, not included in occam.

3.4 BASIC ARCHITECTURE COMPONENTS

Four basic process architecture components are described here and it is shown how these components can be connected together to form typical parallel process configurations:

Funnel	**Array**
Pipe	**Work Router**

3.4.1 The Funnel

Interaction with physical devices can only occur within a single process. In particular, the screen can only be accessed from a single process. We must create a mechanism which receives input from a variety of source processes and concentrates these into a single output channel. The funnel process, illustrated in Fig.3.3, performs this function.

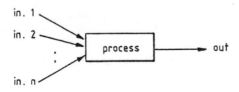

Fig.3.3 Funnel process

```
WHILE TRUE
   SEQ
      ALT
         in.1? data
            SKIP
         in.2?
            SKIP
              .
              .
         in.n? data
            SKIP
      ... process input data
      out! processed.data
```

The occam code to generate this function consists of an endless loop, which receives input from the first available source input channel, processes the input data and outputs the result on channel "out", typically outputting to a screen. (The use of SKIP statements is covered in Chapter 5.)

We may view this funnel process as a multiplexing process to interface with physical output devices.

It will be apparent that we will also require a demultiplexing process to handle **input** from a physical device and its transmission to one of a number of parallel processes (see Fig.3.4).

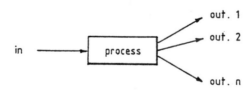

Fig.3.4 Demultiplexing process

```
SEQ
   in? data
   IF
      ... condition 1
         out.1! data
      ... condition 2
         out.2! data
             .
             .
             .
      ... condition n
         out.n! data
```

The corresponding occam code inputs the data and, by means of the conditional IF construct, directs the data to the appropriate output channel.

3.4.2 The Pipe

A pictorial representation of this process is given in Fig.3.5(a). The process simply receives input data on input channel,"in", performs some processing on the data and transmits it to another process via channel "out".

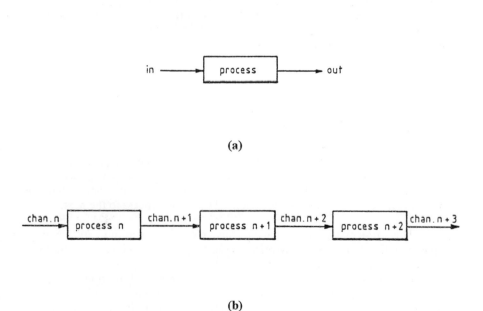

(a)

(b)

Fig.3.5 (a) Pipe process (b) Pipeline arrangement

When connected together in the configuration shown in Fig.3.5(b), we have a pipeline of parallel processes. The code to implement this partial pipeline is as follows:-

```
PAR
  SEQ
    chan.n? input.data
    ... process n
    chan.n1! output.data
  SEQ
    chan.n1? input.data
    ... process n+1
    chan.n2! output.data
  SEQ
    chan.n2? input.data
    ... process n+2
    chan.n3! output.data
```

Fig.3.5(b) illustrates part of a pipeline, conveniently omitting the start and finish processes in order that the corresponding code is simpler. We will deal with the problem of termination of concurrent processes in Chapter 5.

In the operation of a pipeline, a chain of processes is set up. Each process performs' part of the overall computation on the input data and transfers the result to the next process. Subsequent processes each contribute to the overall computation requirement with the result that the final product of the computation is output by the last process in the pipeline.

Now consider the individual actions of process n and process n + 1. At some point in time, process n will be performing computations on the $(k+1)$th input data sample while process n + 1 is dealing with the kth input data sample. This consideration reveals that the throughput of a pipeline is limited by the throughput of the slowest part (or pipe component) of the pipeline.

i.e. processing time for an N-stage pipeline $= N \times \max[t(1),t(2),...,t(N)]$,

where t(i) is the time taken for stage i of the pipeline. In addition, there will be some additional time involved in passing data from one pipe process to the next.

This processing time factor has clear implications for controller implementation and control law generation, in particular. Fig.3.6 illustrates the problem. Input data is processed and output at the sampling rate. However, in this example, it can be seen that the time taken to process the k-th input data sample exceeds three sampling intervals. When the throughput time exceeds the sampling interval in this way, it results in a control law implementation technique which is inconsistent with current design practice and which is unlikely to prove popular.

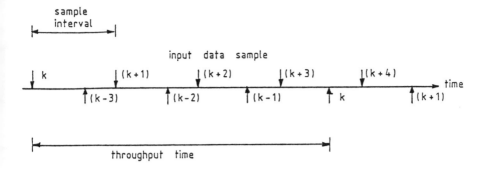

Fig.3.6 Sampling time/throughput relationship

Notwithstanding the throughput time issue, the use of pipelines do seem appropriate for digital signal processing applications where there is a high data rate. This architecture has been adopted in a number of signal processor architectures.

3.4.3 The Array

This may be simply viewed as a two-dimensional version of the pipe, in which data propagates from both West to East and North to South (see Fig.3.7).

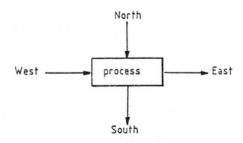

Fig.3.7 Array process

The intention is to integrate this component into the equivalent of a systolic array configuration [4], as illustrated in Fig.3.8. (Suitable modification of the basic element will permit the alternative systolic array configurations given in Fig.3.9.)

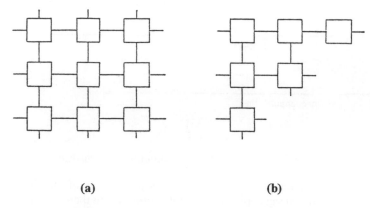

(a)   (b)

**Fig.3.8   (a) 2-dimensional square array
(b) Triangular array**

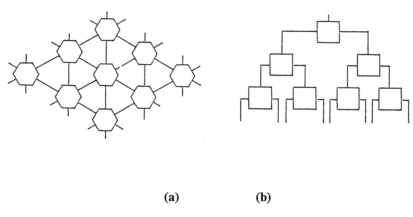

(a)   (b)

**Fig.3.9 (a) 2-dimensional hexagonal array
(b) Binary tree**

Chapman et al.[5] discuss design strategies for implementing systolic and wavefront arrays using occam while Jones [6] describes a matrix multiplication method in occam using the structure given in Fig.3.8(a). A systolic architecture for parallel Kalman filtering is described in Chapter 12.

3.4.4 The Work Router [7]

The role of this component is to monitor input data and either to process the data and return the result or to transfer the data on to another similar component.

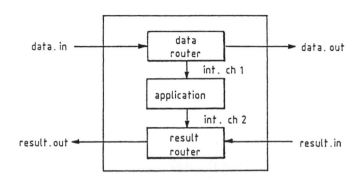

Fig.3.10 Work Router process

In Fig.3.10, data is received on channel "data.in" and is examined by the sub-component "data router". This sub-component decides whether this data is to be transferred to the next work router without modification via output channel "data.out", or whether it is to be processed by the application sub-component. If the latter case is true, after processing, the application sub-component transfers the result to the "result router" sub-component. The "result router" receives input from this internal channel and from the "result.in" channel, routing result data out via the channel "result.out".

These components can be configured as shown in Fig.3.11, where a Controller transmits data along a line of components, one of which will perform the processing. The line is terminated by a Terminator process.

Typical code for the realization of the work router component process is as follows:-

```
PAR
  SEQ
  -- data router
    data.in? data
    ... data router process
    IF
      ... condition 1
        int.ch1! data
      ... condition 2
        data.out! data
  SEQ
  -- application
    int.ch1? data
    ... application process
    int.ch2! result
  SEQ
  -- result router
    ALT
      int.ch2? result
        SKIP
      result.in? result
        SKIP
    ... result router process
    result.out! result
```

The convention of using "--" to prefix a comment is employed here. The three sub-components: data router, application and result router are organised to run in parallel.

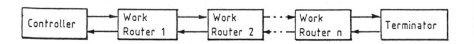

Fig.3.11 Deployment of Work Routers

Methods for "farming" out processes are discussed in [8] and in Chapter 7 an alternative scheme will address the attendant scheduling problems arising from task inter- dependencies associated with this approach.

3.5 FUNCTIONAL DECOMPOSITION

Often a dataflow analysis of the application will reveal a possible application of parallelism along functional lines. Consider, for example, the real-time controller implementation presented in Fig.3.12. An examination of dataflow patterns reveals that this system may be functionally decomposed into five tasks:

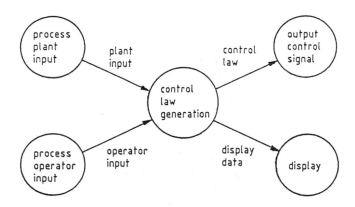

Fig. 3.12   Real-time controller - simplified dataflow analysis

Additional analysis may result in further decomposition of functions. Certainly, in any real-time environment, it is probable that a degree of concurrency will be present in the resulting functions which could be exploited through the application of parallel system design techniques. A more detailed study follows in the next Chapter.

3.6 HARDWARE CONFIGURATION

Up to this point, no consideration has been given to hardware realisation. It is well-known that the occam programming language is hosted by the INMOS transputer device. One of the strengths of occam is that, irrespective of the target hardware, it allows the designer to start with any algorithm and investigate its implementation on a variety of different architectures.

Up to now, we have referred to "processes" in connection with occam program construction and not to "processors". The latter term is the **physical** division of a task while the first term is the **logical** division of a task. The reason for our concentration on the logical component is that it is possible to allocate several processes to one processor; indeed, it is possible to realise an entire occam program of many processes on a single processor. Occam provides the means for the programmer to map a program comprising many processes onto a specific number of processors and to allocate specific processes to individual processors.

The recommended approach, [7], to parallel system design using occam, is to decompose the problem to a greater, rather than lesser extent, creating more logical processes than physical processors. This provides more freedom in the implementation, since it is easier to group processes than sub-divide them once a design is established.

Factors to be considered in deciding the physical processor configuration include:-

Processor communication - Speed, amount of data to be transferred and the number of physical links.

Processor loading   - equitable distribution of computation load.

Processor memory size   - consideration of the use of fast on-chip memory for program and data storage.

3.7 SUMMARY

Occam enables an application to be described as a collection of concurrent processes which communicate using channels. Programs are constructed from processes combined together using constructors. The primitive processes of input, output and assignment form the lowest level of process in a program. An occam program may be implemented on a network of interconnected computers, each executing one or more of the concurrent processes. The language provides the means of realising a system in many different ways, thus enabling the designer to choose the most appropriate implementation with respect to performance, cost and available technology.

ACKNOWLEDGEMENTS

Dr. D.I. Jones, P. Entwistle, D. Lawrie, F. Garcia and H. Thompson (members of the Bangor Control Software Group) have all contributed useful ideas and comments during the development of this Chapter. Their invaluable assistance is gratefully acknowledged.

REFERENCES

1.'Occam Programming Manual', 1984, INMOS Ltd, Prentice Hall.

2.Pountain, D., 1988, "A Tutorial Introduction to OCCAM Programming", Blackwell Ltd.

3.Hoare, C.A.R., 1985, "Communicating Sequential Processes", Prentice Hall International.

4.May, D., "Communicating Processes and OCCAM", INMOS Technical Note 20.

5.Chapman, R., Durrani, T.S. and Willey, T., 1985, "Design Strategies for Implementing Systolic and Wavefront Arrays Using OCCAM", Proceedings of the IEEE International Conference on Acoustics, Speech and Signal Processing, Florida, U.S.A., vol.1, pp. 292-295.

6.Jones, G., 1985, "Programming in OCCAM", Programming Research Group Technical Monograph PRG-43, University of Oxford.

7.Mattos, P., "Program Design for Concurrent Systems", INMOS Technical Note 5.

8.May, D. and R. Shepherd, R., "Communicating Process Computers", INMOS Technical Note 22.

Chapter 4

Occam structures in control

Dr. D.I. Jones

4.1 INTRODUCTION

As we have seen, parallel processing seeks to reduce the time taken to compute a given task. This is done by distributing the task over a number of co-operating processors, ideally in such a way that the available processors are fully utilised and the speed-up is proportional to their number.

It is desirable that the task distribution is specified in a high-level language in order to reduce the time required for software development and maintenance. In the last Chapter we saw that INMOS have sought to achieve this in the design of the occam language.

Furthermore, the transputer is a microprocessor which is specifically designed for compatibility with occam code, having high speed serial duplex links to implement communication channels and a hardware scheduler to support the process model. Thus the transfer of code from the development environment to the target system should be efficient and trouble-free.

In this Chapter, some examples are given which illustrate the use of the occam programming language in control applications. The three examples are:

    (a) Numerical integration
    (b) Gradient minimisation with array line search
    (c) A real-time control system.

The examples illustrate how some of the parallel architectures introduced in the last Chapter are applied in a control engineering context. The structure and dataflow which characterise each case are presented and outline code is used to show how they may be represented in occam.

The examples are not fully-developed case studies. Rather they are intended to demonstrate that numerical algorithms for real-time control and computer aided design may be configured for multiprocessor systems using the occam approach. Also, they will serve to illustrate some of the problems encountered when attempting to distribute a computational task over more than one processor. Usually this will lead to the desired proportionality between speed-up and number of processors not being achieved.

4.2 NUMERICAL INTEGRATION

The simulation of dynamic systems on digital computers is done by means of numerical integration. Some techniques for CAD of control systems by means of nonlinear optimisation require repeated system simulation which is a heavy computational burden [1]. Some system simulations are high order and nonlinear yet must be computed at high speed. An example is given by Krosel & Milner [2] where a real-time simulation is to be used as a substitute for a gas turbine engine while testing digital controllers. In this latter case, dedicated and portable hardware is required.

Several schemes have been suggested for parallel methods of numerical integration - some of these are reviewed by Franklin [3]. An obvious method is to divide the system derivative functions between the available processors but this requires careful balancing of the workload so that none of the processors are left idle.

Another technique suggested by Miranker & Liniger [4] is to adapt Adams-Bashforth predictor-corrector formulae for parallel processing. The set of ordinary differential equations to be solved is:

$$\mathbf{x} = f(\mathbf{x,u},t)$$

$$(4.1)$$

The example is confined to the second-order predictor- corrector formulae:

$$x^p_{n+1} = x^c_n + h/2[3f^c_n - f^c_{n-1}]$$

$$(4.2a)$$

$$x^c_{n+1} = x^c_n + h/2\,[f^p_{n+1} + f^c_n]$$

$$(4.2b)$$

where:

x_n = an approximation to $\mathbf{x}$ at time t_n

x^p_n = predicted value of x_n

x^c_n = corrected value of x_n

$f^p_n = f(x^p_n, t_n)$ ⎤ i.e. the derivative function evaluated at time t_n using
$\quad\quad\quad\quad\quad$ ⎬ the predicted and corrected values of x_n respectively
$f^c_n = f(x^c_n, t_n)$ ⎦

h = time step

The standard method is strictly sequential:

$$x^P_{n+1} \rightarrow f^P_{n+1} \rightarrow x^c_{n+1} \rightarrow f^c_{n+1} \rightarrow \text{etc.}$$

Miranker & Liniger modify the formulae to :

$$x^P_{n+1} = x^c_{n-1} + 2\,h\,f^P_n$$

(4.3a)

$$x^c_n = x^c_{n-1} + (h/2)\,[\,f^P_n + f^c_{n-1}\,]$$

(4.3b)

where the sequence of computation is divided and each of its two parts may be simultaneously executed:

$$x^P_{n+1} \rightarrow f^P_{n+1} \qquad\qquad x^c_n \rightarrow f^c_n$$

However, each process requires data calculated by the other and this coincides with the occam model of communicating sequential processes. The occam structure is shown in Fig.4.1 and is written:

```
CHAN m.to.p, m.to.c, c.to.m, p.to.c, c.to.p:
PAR
  Master ( m.to.p, m.to.c, c.to.m )
  Predictor ( m.to.p, p.to.c, c.to.p )
  Corrector ( p.to.c, c.to.p, c.to.m, m.to.c)
```

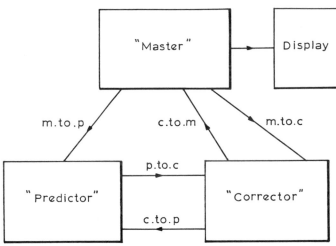

Fig.4.1 Structure of processes defining a parallel scheme for numerical integration.

The "Master" process acts rather like a demultiplexer (see Chapter 3.4.1), passing control values (u) down channels m.to.p and m.to.c to the other processes. Processes "Predictor" and "Corrector" are similar in structure, evaluating equations (4.3a) and (4.3b), respectively, and exchanging data when required to do so.

Process "Corrector" is written:

```
WHILE NOT end.flag
  SEQ
    m.to.p ? u        -- control value from "Master"
    ...calculate fP_n
    PAR
      p.to.c ! fP_n  -- predicted derivative to
                     --           "Corrector"
      ...calculate xP_n+1
    c.to.p ? xC_n    -- corrected state from "Corrector
```

This process is executed repeatedly until the Boolean variable 'end.flag' becomes true. On receipt of a control value (u_n) from "Master", process "Predictor" first computes the predicted derivative, f^P_n, which it then passes along channel p.to.c to "Corrector" while itself going on to calculate the predicted state x^P_{n+1}. Under the occam rules, it then waits for a corrected state, x^c_n, to come along channel c.to.p from "Corrector" and on receipt of this information loops back to the start to wait for another control value.

Since the equations for the two processors involve approximately the same amount of arithmetic, the partitioning is well balanced and a speed-up of almost double may be expected. It is possible to extend the method to a greater number of processors by using higher order formulae. Krosel & Milner report satisfactory accuracy and speed-up but decreasing stability limits with eight processors.

This is an example of a sequential algorithm being converted into parallel form. In this case its numerical properties have been investigated in some detail by Miranker & Liniger. However, in general, heuristic adaptation of algorithms is a dangerous procedure.

4.3 GRADIENT MINIMISATION WITH ARRAY LINE SEARCH

Optimisation by means of a search method is a well known technique in CACSD (Computer Aided Control System Design) and has been proposed for on-line adaptive control [5]. Search methods involve minimising an objective function with respect to a number of parameters, and an important component is the univariate line search. The objective function is minimised with respect to a single scalar parameter, alpha, along a given set of search directions in multi-dimensional space.

The essence of this example is to investigate how all the evaluations of the objective function can be carried out in parallel by using occam to define a row of processes for the computation. This is illustrated by applying steepest descent directions for minimising the quadratic function:

$$V = f(x) = 2x_1^2 + 1.5x_2^2 + 2x_1x_2 + x_1 + x_2 + 3$$

(4.4)

The gradients of V are:

$$g_1 = (\delta f(x)/\delta x_1) = 4x_1 + 2x_2 + 1$$

(4.5a)

$$g_2 = (\delta f(x)/\delta x_2) = 3x_1 + 2x_2 + 1$$

(4.5b)

For a minimum of f(x), $g_1 = g_2 = 0$ yielding:

$$x_{min} = [-0.125\ -0.250]\ \text{and}\ f(x_{min}) = 2.81250.$$

Starting from an initial guess for x_1 and x_2, the recursion:

$$x_{k+1} = x_k + \alpha(-g_k)$$

(4.6)

is used to search for the minimum. The line search along the row of processors is a simple doubling of α from the initial point, and the least value found is chosen as the start of the next search.

Fig.4.2 shows an arrangement of replicated processes which all execute in parallel. In general each "Master()" process in the row is interlinked to left and right, with process "Overseer" to coordinate the flow of data into the chain. The architecture is similar to the Work-router (Chapter 3.4.4), though the data flow is simpler.

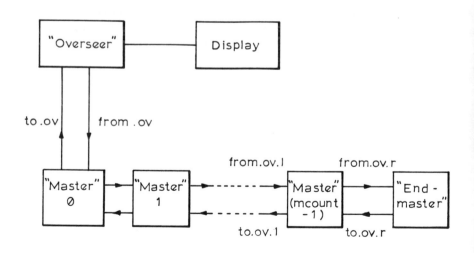

Fig.4.2 Structure of processes for a parallel line search

The outline action is as follows:

(i) A value of α and trial values of x are passed from "Overseer" to "Master(0)" and propagated up the chain to "Endmaster". The value of α is doubled by each successive processor.

(ii) Each "Master()" process computes a value of the objective function ,V, for the given value of α, then passes it to the left down the chain to "Overseer".

(iii) Process "Overseer" selects the least value of V and the trial point associated with it becomes the starting value of x for the next iteration of the algorithm.

The occam structure is:

```
DEF mcount=no.Master.processes:
CHAN to.ov[mcount],from.ov[mcount]:
PAR
  Overseer(from.ov[0],to.ov[0])
  PAR j=[0 FOR mcount-1]
    Master(from.ov[j],to.ov[j],from.ov[j+1],to.ov[j+1])
  Endmaster(from.ov[mcount-1],to.ov[mcount-1])
```

(A replicated PAR statement is used on the 5th line of the above code example. The use of **replicators** is covered in Chapter 5.12).

It is instructive to look closer at stage (ii) above since it is clear that each "Master()" process must carry out its own computation while, in parallel, monitoring processes to the right for values of V being passed down the chain. To accommodate this we write "Master()" as a sequential and an alternative process operating in parallel:

```
PROC Master( )=
  SEQ
    ... take in α and trial x on channel from.ov.1[
    PAR
```

(a)
```
      SEQ
        ... i)    calculate gradients g at given x₁,
        ... ii)   calculate new trial values of x₁, x₂
                  with allocated α value according to
                      xnew := xold + α(-g).
        ... iii)  calculate final function value
                      V = f(xnew)
      WHILE going
      ALT
```

Where the equations are:

(a)
- i) calculate gradients g at given x_1,
- ii) calculate new trial values of x_1, x_2 with allocated α value according to $x_{new} := x_{old} + \alpha(-g)$.
- iii) calculate final function value $V = f(x_{new})$

(b)
- i) monitor "Master()" processes to th right and if any value of V appears, send it on down towards "Overseer".
- ii) if (a) above is ready, send the val of V to "Overseer"
- iii) monitor the "Master()" process to t left for reset flag; on receipt going:=FALSE

First, note that process (b) still operates once (a) has terminated. Secondly, only one of the three processes in (b) is chosen to execute at any time. Usually this will be b(i), except for the occasion when this processor communicates its own value of V down the chain, i.e. b(ii). Process (b) continues to be active until it is deliberately reset, in b(iii), to the start of another main iteration of the algorithm.

Process "Overseer" exists to select the minimum value of V, coordinate the chain and handle display and storage.

A program was written having 8 "Master()" processes. The progress of the minimisation is illustrated in Fig.4.3, from an initial guess of [-0.125, 0.5].

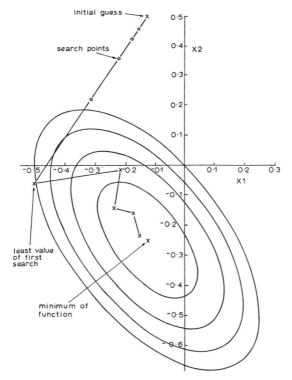

**Fig.4.3 Line searches for a minimum of a quadratic
function of two variables**

Obviously this example may be extended in a straight- forward manner by calculating conjugate gradients, using a longer line search etc., but other techniques for achieving greater parallelism could be proposed such as another "Master()" chain to evaluate another line search (concurrently) along some other direction.

It should be noted that the use of eight processors does not imply a speed-up factor of eight, even if the communication overhead is considered negligible. This is because, at each iteration, the calculation of the gradients (eqns. 4.5) is duplicated within all the "Master()" processes. Thus the speed-up ratio will depend on the relative computation times of the gradients and the objective function. Also, it should be noted that a weakness of this architecture is the requirement for all communication to pass through the first "Master" process in the chain. This might form a bottleneck in some circumstances.

Combining examples 1 and 2 illustrates the possibility of hierarchy in parallel architectures, where each of the function evaluations in example 2 could be a numerical integration as performed in example 1; hence the common "Master" nomenclature used.

4.4 A REAL-TIME CONTROL SYSTEM

This example is founded on a control system for a microgravity isolation mount [6] and is fairly representative of the functions required of a real-time controller.

The application itself is concerned with the control of an experimental platform situated in the weightless (microgravity) environment of Earth orbit. The platform is free to move within a limited volume inside a spacecraft. Constraints on its movement are provided, in six degrees of freedom, by means of a non-contact magnetic suspension system. The bandwidths of the control loops are set such that the platform follows long-term motion of the spacecraft but rejects higher frequency vibration present on the spacecraft structure.

There are three independent control loops. Each loop operates in a plane to control the linear motion of the platform along one axis and its angular motion (ψ) about a second axis - see Fig.4.4.

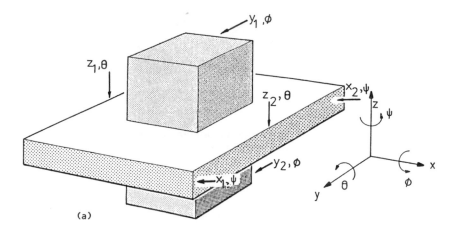

e.g.   actuators sited at gaps x_1 and x_2 control
       rectilinear motion in x and angular motion in ψ.

Fig.4.4 Outline of microgravity isolation mount

The gap between the platform and its enclosure is sensed at two points - the sum signal is a measure of mean position while the difference signal is a measure of angle. The required form of control loop is shown in Fig.4.5, the output being force and torque signals which are directed to appropriate actuators.

On top of this there are several other operational requirements which can be represented for the sake of this example as 'loop control'. For instance, if the gap between the platform and its enclosure becomes too small, a warning is given to the operator and a clamping system is activated to hold the platform. The operator must also be able to reset the system.

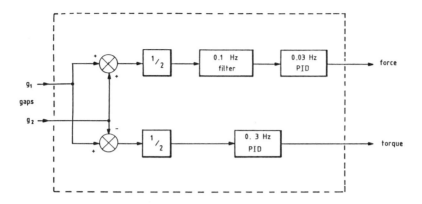

Fig.4.5 Form of one control loop for the microgravity isolation mount

Clearly, we have a requirement for measuring sensor signals, dynamic compensation and control signal output. Monitoring and user interaction are also part of the overall system. This has a natural functional decomposition as described in Chapter 3.5 and can be represented by the block diagram of Fig.4.6.

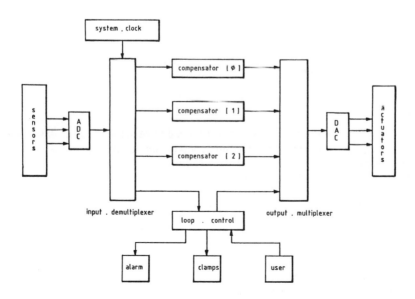

Fig. 4.6 Structure of the control system

This is easily structured in occam:

```
PAR
   ... System.clock
   ... Input.demultiplexer
   ... Output.multiplexer
   ... Loop.control
   PAR i= [0 FOR 3]
      Compensator [i]        -- three identical compensators
```

The flow of data between the processes, and its synchronisation, is regulated by the occam channel protocol. The System.clock provides a fixed sampling interval. At each sample time the Input.demultiplexer inputs six sensor signals from the ADC. Then the measured values are dispersed to the compensator processes which send their output to the Output.multiplexer. Once all six control values are present they are transferred to the DAC. Sensor inputs are also sent to Loop.control which checks for violation of gap limits and activates the alarm and clamp system, if necessary. It also monitors user input for a reset signal.

The System.clock is easily coded in occam and is supported in the T414 transputer by a 1 microsecond resolution, 32-bit real-time clock:

```
PROC System.clock (Clock.to.Demux)=
... initialisation
   WHILE TRUE
      SEQ
         --set t to current value of clock
         timer ? t
         --trigger the ADC sample
         Clock.to.Demux ! ANY
         --wait until sample.interval has passed before
         --                                        proceeding
         timer ? AFTER (t + sample.interval):
```

The Input.demultiplexer will now proceed to read six words of data (one for each sensor) from the ADC along the single input channel, then disperse them to the waiting processes. Henceforth, channel declarations will be omitted but are implied in the text of the occam code.

```
PROC Input.demultiplexer(  )=
...initialisation
  WHILE TRUE
    SEQ
      --await trigger
      Clock.to.Demux ? ANY
      ... read several channels of ADC into gap.values[ ]
      PAR
        PAR i= [0 FOR 3]
          SEQ j= [0 FOR 2]
            --disperse signals
            Demux.to.comp[i] ! gap.values[(2*i)+j]
        SEQ k= [0 FOR 6]
          --also to Loop.control
          Demux.to.Loop.con ! gap.values[k]  :
```

Providing the sample interval is of sufficient length, all other processes will now be awaiting data input. Thus the compensator processes will take the form:

```
PROC Compensator[ ] (      )=
...initialisation
  WHILE TRUE
    SEQ
      --receive measured values
      Demux.to.comp ? first.gap;second.gap
      ... compute Force[ ]
      ... compute Torque[ ]
      --send the output
      Comp.to.mux ! Force.Torque.values  :
```

Meanwhile, the Loop.control process decides whether the sensor inputs are a cause for alarm. The upper half of the ALT construct will always be executed at each sample time. In normal operation the value of shutdown will be FALSE and this will be transmitted to Output.multiplexer to validate the control signals. If the gap limits are violated the alarm is sounded and a TRUE shutdown signal sent which inhibits the control signal output.

In order to recover from a shutdown situation, the second half of the ALT construct monitors the (user) reset channel. An input from the user will cancel the alarm, and reset shutdown to FALSE.

```
PROC Loop.control (    )=
SEQ
  ...initialisation
  shutdown:=FALSE
  WHILE TRUE
    ALT
      Demux.to.loop.con ? gap.values
        SEQ
          IF
            any.gap.value > limit      --shutdown necessary
              SEQ
                clamps ! close          --close clamps
                alarm ! alarm.on        --and sound alarm
                shutdown := TRUE
            Loop.control.to.mux ! shutdown     -- inhibit or
                                               -- validate
      user ? ANY                        --user reset ?
        SEQ
          clamps ! open
          alarm ! alarm.off
          shutdown := FALSE     :
```

Finally, at each sample time, process Output.multiplexer will collect the output signals **and** the state of the shutdown signal. If the latter is acceptable then the output signals are transferred to the DAC along the single output channel. Otherwise a zero control output is sent instead.

```
PROC Output.multiplexer (    )=
...initialisation
  WHILE TRUE
    SEQ
      PAR
        Loop.con.to.Mux ? shutdown    --shutdown necessary?
        --will not proceed until all values present
        PAR j= [0 FOR 3]
          Comp.to.mux[j] ? Force.Torque.values
      IF
        NOT shutdown
          ...send Force.Torque.values to
                          Output.demultiplexer
        shutdown
          ...send all zeros to Output.demultiplexer    :
```

Note that the loop continues to function normally even during shutdown but the output signal is inhibited. This feature allows communication across all the channels to take place as normal thus avoiding the risk of deadlock.

The example given above is certainly not the only way, and perhaps not the best way, to structure this controller. Nevertheless it does demonstrate the natural affinity of occam with the underlying hardware. This makes it relatively straightforward to map between processes and processors, perhaps more so for a systems engineer than a conventional programmer. Occam encourages early definition of the dataflow involved in a particular application and the structure diagrams are a valuable aid to software construction. In turn this encourages overall system descriptions in pseudo-code to be produced **before** becoming involved in the details of the internal processes. The obvious decomposition of a system in this way is not always the best strategy. For instance, in Jones and Entwistle [7], there is an example where the 'natural' structure of the hardware does not draw the optimum parallelism out of the task to be computed.

4.5 CONCLUSIONS

This Chapter has outlined some of the features of the occam language and how it may be used in control applications. The recent availability of occam2, described in the next Chapter has greatly eased the problems of data types and made numerical expressions easier to code.

ACKNOWLEDGEMENT

This material is partly based on a paper published by the Institute of Measurement and Control [8] and is included with their permission.

REFERENCES

1.Jones, D.I. and Finch, J.W., 1984, " Comparison of optimization algorithms", Int.J.Control, vol.40 , pp. 747-761.

2.Krosel, S.M. and Milner, E.J., 1982, "Application of integration algorithms in a parallel processing environment for the simulation of jet engines", Proc.IEEE Annual Simulation Symposium, 1982, pp. 121-143.

3.Franklin, M.A., 1978, "Parallel solution of ordinary differential equations", IEEE Trans. Computers, C-27, pp. 413-430.

4.Miranker, W.L. and Liniger, W.M., 1967, "Parallel methods for the numerical integration of ordinary differential equations", Math.Comp., vol. 21, pp. 303-320.

5.Travassos, R. and Kaufman, H., 1980, "Impact of parallel computers on adaptive flight control", Proc.JACC San Francisco, 1980, Paper WP1-8.

6.Jones, D.I., Owens, A.R., Owen, R.G., 1987, "A microgravity isolation mount", Acta Astronautica, vol. 5/6.

7.Jones, D.I., Entwistle, P.M., 1986, "A parallel processor approach to the inverse dynamics problem of a robot manipulator", Proc. 10th Annual Workshop on Microcomputer Applications, University of Strathclyde, September, 1986.

8.Jones, D.I., 1985, "Occam structures in control applications", Trans. Inst. Meas. Control, vol. 7, pp. 222-227.

Chapter 5

Programming in occam

Dr. P.J. Fleming

5.1 INTRODUCTION

In this Chapter we examine the occam programming language in more detail, highlighting the occam2 version of the language. We have three objectives in mind:-

(a) to provide a fuller introduction to the nature of the software design task,

(b) to highlight common problems often encountered by newcomers to parallel programming and to occam, in particular, and

(c) to provide material sufficient for a full appreciation of programming examples in later Chapters.

A more formal description of the language appears in [1], [2], while Pountain [3] provides a very useful and extended tutorial introduction.

5.2 PRIMITIVE PROCESSES

In addition to the three processes:-

Assignment   v : = e,
Input   c ? v, and
Output   c ! e,

occam has two special processes called SKIP and STOP.

SKIP is a process that does nothing and then terminates. It might be used in partially completed code in place of a process to be included later. There are also occasions when we require nothing to happen, but the syntax of occam requires a process to be present. We have already seen the role of SKIP statements in the Funnel and Work Router examples of Chapter 3.4.4 to complete the syntax of ALT constructs.

STOP is a process that also does nothing, but, unlike SKIP, it does not terminate. Again, it might be used in partially completed code in place of a process to be included later.

When STOP is executed within a sequential process, that process is stopped. Nothing more can happen within that process. Further, any process which needs to communicate with the 'stopped' process will itself never finish. The effect of a STOP is therefore liable to propagate in this way. This is similar to what happens when processes become deadlocked.

A process which completes all its actions is said to **terminate**.

5.3 TYPES

In occam, the names of data objects can be any length, consisting of a sequence of alphabetic characters, decimal digits and dots (.), the first of which must be an alphabetic character. Upper and lower case are dis- tinguished by occam.

5.3.1 Elementary Data

The following elementary data types are provided:-

INT	a signed integer value
BYTE	an integer value between 0 and 255, (often used to represent characters)
BOOL	a Boolean logical value, i.e. TRUE or FALSE,

and are declared thus:-

```
INT n:
BYTE char:
BOOL level:
```

An implementation of occam may also provide extra data types as extensions, e.g. INT16, INT32, INT64, REAL32 and REAL64. A signed integer value represented in 2's complement form using n bits is of type INTn. A signed real value is of type REAL32 or REAL64.

5.3.2 Representation of Characters

Occam does not have a data type to represent characters or character strings. Instead, characters are represented as numbers of type BYTE and character strings as arrays of numbers of type BYTE.

A single character contained in single quotes, e.g. 'a', is translated into a one byte number. Similarly, a text string written in double quotes, e.g. "control", is translated into an array of bytes. Occam uses the ASCII standard code with a guaranteed subset. Any character can be represented by an asterisk followed by its code in hexadecimal notation, where hexadecimal notation is # followed by two hexadecimal digits. Certain characters are represented as follows:-

*c	carriage return
*n	new line
*t	horizontal tabulate

5.3.3 Constants and Abbreviations

Constants are specified thus:- VAL type name IS value:

e.g.   VAL INT max IS 100:

The above use of VAL is a special case of a more general device known as an abbreviation which enables a name to be given to any occam expression:-

VAL REAL32 lag IS (t1 + t2)/(t1 * t2):

Any variables in the expression must remain constant throughout the scope of the abbreviation. An abbreviation thus behaves like a constant throughout its scope. An explanation of scope follows in the next Section.

5.3.4 Channels

Channels are all of the type:-

CHAN OF protocol name:

Every input and output on a channel must be compatible with the protocol of the channel. Hence it is necessary to specify the data type and structure of the values to be transmitted on a channel. Here is a simple kind of protocol:-

CHAN OF INT adc1:

As protocol requirements become more complex, leading to the communication of a sequence of simple protocols, it is convenient to include such a sequence in a protocol definition such as :-

PROTOCOL Mix IS INT ; BYTE ; BOOL:
CHAN OF Mix ch1:

There also exists a variant protocol, which enables the specification of a set of different protocols, any one of which may be used when communicating on the assigned channel.

5.3.5 Timers

The provision of a TIMER type is, of course, important in real-time programming. This data object behaves like a channel which can only provide input. The input value is the current time represented as a value of type INT. The 'count' of the clock will be implementation-dependent.

Example:-

```
TIMER clock:
INT time:
SEQ
   clock? time
```

In this simple process, the current time is input from "clock" and assigned to "time".

5.4 SCOPE

In the above type declaration examples it will have been noted that each declaration ends with a colon. The effect of the colon is to join the declaration to the process which follows it. To enforce this connection, declarations are indented to the same level as the process, e.g.

```
CHAN OF INT adc1,adc2:
PAR
  INT data1:
  SEQ
    adc1? data1
    ... process data1
  INT data2:
  SEQ
    adc2? data2
    ... process data2
```

Each name used in an occam program must be declared before it can be used. Variables, channels and other named objects are local to the process which immediately follows their declaration. In the above example, "data1" exists only within the first SEQ process and "data2" exists only within the second.

In the following example, the same name, "data", may be used for a different object with a different scope:

```
PAR
  INT data:
  SEQ
    adc1? data
    ... process data
  INT data:
  SEQ
    adc2? data
    ... process data
```

Here each "data" is local to its occam process. Altering the value of "data" in the first process has no effect on the second. Remember that occam does not permit the use of shared variables.

If, inside the scope of a variable, another variable is declared with the same name, then within its own scope the new variable replaces the original. The original object is said to be masked by the new object. Consider, for example:

```
INT data:
SEQ
  adc1? data
  ... process data
  INT data:
  SEQ
    adc2? data
    ... process data
```

Input from "adc2" is communicated to the second "data". The first "data" cannot be accessed from the nested SEQ process.

Note, that, upon declaration, a variable is **not** initialised to zero. Therefore, once a process is terminated, its local variables become undefined and must be re-initialised upon subsequent execution. For a variable to retain its value from one execution of a process to another, it must be declared in an outer scope.

5.5 ARRAY DATA TYPE

An array is a device for structuring data objects in occam. It is a group of data objects of the same type, where these objects can be any one of the elementary data types, e.g.

[10] REAL32 omega: -- an array of 10 reals called omega
[4] CHAN OF INT adc: -- an array of 4 channels called adc
[6] BOOL flag: -- an array of 6 Booleans called flag

The size of an array is fixed at compilation time.

An array variable is referenced by stating the array name followed by the subscript within square brackets. Subscripts start at **zero**. Components of array variables behave like ordinary variables.

Examples:

omega [0] -- the first integer in omega
adc [3] -- the fourth and last channel of adc

freq : = omega [0] + 1

A whole array can be transmitted to another process thus:-

```
PAR
   chan! omega
   chan? alpha
```

where omega and alpha are arrays of the same type and size.

Occam supports multidimensional arrays. For example, a 2-dimensional array is declared as:-

[5][5] REAL32 matA:

5.6 EXPRESSIONS

5.6.1 Real and Integer Arithmetic

The operators +, -, *, /, REM represent the arithmetic sum, difference, product, quotient and remainder respectively. Both operands of an operator must be of the same type; the result is of the same type as the operands.

It is possible to perform type conversion. For example, if "setpoint" and "diff" had been declared as INTEGER and "signal" as BYTE, we could have the following expression:

diff : = setpoint - (INT signal)

Modulo arithmetic can be performed using the operators:

PLUS, MINUS and TIMES.

All operators have the same priority. Parentheses must, therefore, be used in complex expressions.

5.6.2 Booleans

The Boolean constants are TRUE and FALSE and the operators are AND, OR and NOT.

The relational operators =, < >, >, <, > =, < = yield a Boolean value,

e.g.   (n < > 0) is TRUE if n is non-zero and
(n > = 0) is FALSE if n is negative.

5.6.3 Additional Features

Other features involving expressions include bitwise and shift operators. The SIZE operator determines the size of an array and the MOSTPOS and MOSTNEG operators define the most positive and negative integers respectively.

The operator AFTER is often used in conjunction with a variable representing time to cause a delay:

```
TIMER clock:
INT current.time,delay:
SEQ
  clock? current.time
  clock? AFTER current.time PLUS delay
```

This has the effect of first inputting from "clock" the current time. In the succeeding statement, no variable has its value changed. Instead, the value from "clock" is compared with the value of the expression, effecting a delay proportional to the integer value represented by "delay".

5.7 PROCEDURES

Names may be given to processes by means of PROC declarations, followed by a process, called the procedure body:-

PROC delay ()
... procedure body

The empty parentheses denote that this procedure has no parameters. In general, a procedure may have a list of formal parameters which are included in parentheses following its name declaration, e.g.

```
PROC output.char ([] BYTE string, CHAN OF BYTE ch, INT i)
  ch! string [i]
          .
          .
          .
BYTE st1[7]:
INT n:
CHAN OF BYTE ch1:
  st1 := "control"
  n := 4
  output.char (st1, ch1, n)
```

We see from this example that channels and arrays can be passed as parameters as well as simple variables. The **instance** of the procedure - output.char (st1,ch1,n) - causes the character "r", the 5th letter of "control", to be output on channel "ch1", remembering that array subscripts start at zero.

The body of a procedure is executed whenever its name occurs in a program. It is as though the body of the procedure had been substituted for the name. The occurrence of a procedure name is known as an **instance** of a procedure.

The parameter transmission mechanism is 'call by reference'. That is, the actual parameter behaves as though it replaces the formal parameter throughout the procedure. Any change that is made to the formal parameter is automatically made to the actual parameter.

Occam also has **functions**. A function is a special kind of process which returns a result, e.g.

c := max(a,b)

where max is a function returning the maximum of two values.

5.8 SEQUENTIAL AND PARALLEL PROCESSES

5.8.1 SEQ and PAR Constructs

We have seen in Chapter 3 how an occam program is based on the concept of communicating sequential processes. The following example of the sequential construct is a simple buffer, which repeatedly inputs a value from channel "in" and outputs it to channel "out".

```
CHAN OF INT in,out:
WHILE TRUE
  INT x :
  SEQ
    in? x
    out! x
```

The parallel construct is often used to combine sequential processes, as in the following example (see Fig.5.1), where it combines two simple buffer processes to form a buffer which can hold two values:-

```
CHAN OF INT in,out,ch:
PAR
  WHILE TRUE
    INT x:
    SEQ
      in? x
      ch! x
  WHILE TRUE
    INT x:
    SEQ
      ch? x
      out! x
```

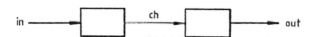

Fig: 5.1 Two simple buffer processes

This example also demonstrates the mechanism provided by occam for the hierarchical decomposition of processes. Since the parallel process itself consists of two sequential processes it may be depicted, as in Fig.5.2(a), as one process connected to two channels or, as in Fig.5.2(b), in its decomposed state of two processes connected by a channel.

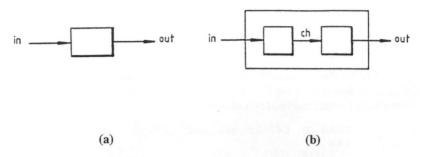

(a)   (b)

**Fig. 5.2   (a) Abstracted view of the two-buffer process
(b) Detailed view of (a).**

One method of hierarchical problem decomposition uses only the PAR construct and channels until the individual processes are as simple as possible. This produces a high degree of concurrency with processes synchronizing only when communication takes place.

Another method uses the SEQ construct to combine parallel constructs, representing the action of a number of processes which all synchronise after each step. This 'double buffer' is an example:-

```
INT x,y:
CHAN OF INT in,out:
SEQ
   in? y
   WHILE TRUE
   SEQ
      PAR
         in? x
         out! y
      PAR
         out! x
         in?  y
```

This example uses two variables, "x" and "y" to allow input and output in Fig.5.3 to proceed concurrently.

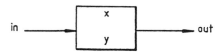

Fig.5.3 Double buffer process

5.8.2 Prioritized PAR

Preceding a PAR construct with the word PRI has the effect of assigning a priority to the processes governed by that construct. The level of priority is determined by the textual order of the processes, the first having highest priority.

This finds use, for example, in real-time applications where it is important to service a particular peripheral quickly:-

```
INT any:
CHAN OF INT alarm:
PRI PAR
  SEQ
    alarm? any
    ... service alarm
  SEQ
    ...another process
```

Here, should any contention arise, the process which services an alarm signal has priority over any other process. Possible contention exists when the number of channels ready to receive input exceeds the number of available processors.

5.9 DEADLOCK

It is pertinent at this point to highlight a recurring problem in concurrent program design: deadlock. We will demonstrate this state by means of two simple examples.

5.9.1 Non-concurrency of Communicating Processes

```
Example:
    INT a,b:
    CHAN OF INT ch:
    SEQ                        -- <<<
      SEQ
        ch? a
        ... process 1
      SEQ
        ch! b
        ... process 2
```

In this example, the first of the nested SEQ processes is programmed to input "a" on channel "ch" and process it. The second of the nested SEQ processes is programmed to output "b" on "ch" and do some processing. However the desired data transmission cannot take place because output on "ch" is programmed to occur in sequence **after** input on that channel.

This is inconsistent with the occam implementation of channels, which requires that data be transmitted via channels between concurrent processes when each process is ready for transmission to take place.

This condition is known as **deadlock,** since execution of the first nested SEQ process cannot proceed until transmission over channel "ch" is successfully completed. The code can be rectified by replacing the 'arrowed' SEQ construct with a PAR construct, thus creating concurrency for the two communicating processes.

5.9.2 Crossed Channels

Example (see Fig. 5.4):

```
        CHAN OF INT ch1,ch2:
        PAR
          -- process 1
          INT a:
          SEQ
            ch1? a
            ch2! 2
          -- process 2
          INT b:
          SEQ
            ch2? b
            ch1! 3
```

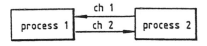

Fig.5.4 Crossed channels example

Once again we have a deadlock situation because both processes are patiently waiting for input data. Since each process is waiting for the other to output, neither can proceed to make the necessary output.

Re-ordering process 2 resolves the problem:-

```
-- process 2
INT b:
SEQ
   ch1!  3
   ch2?  b
```

The importance of attention to potential deadlock situations cannot be over-emphasised. Correct sequencing of code will ensure that two parallel processes are never each waiting for sequentially later output from the other.

Simple examples have been used to illustrate potential difficulties here. However, manifestations of deadlock are often embedded in more complex processes.

5.10 REPETITIVE AND CONDITIONAL PROCESSES

Universal requirements of programming languages are looping and decision-making constructs. Occam has two kinds of looping facility:

(a) repeat for a specified number of times, and
(b) repeat while a given condition holds.

We will meet (a) in Section 5.12. Although not formally introduced, we have already encountered type (b) - the WHILE statement - elsewhere.

Consider a variant of the first example in Section 5.8:

```
INT x:
CHAN OF INT in,out:
SEQ
  x := O
  WHILE x >= 0
    SEQ
      in? x
      out! x
```

This WHILE loop executes by testing that "x" is non-negative and then, provided that this condition is TRUE, executing the body. When the body has terminated, the condition is re-tested, so that the body is executed a number of times in sequence. The loop terminates when the condition is tested and found to be FALSE.

One form of decision-making construct is the IF construct. This construct contains a number of processes, each headed by a condition. Each condition is inspected and the **first** one, whose test is true, is executed. The IF construct is therefore priority structured.

Example:

```
INT x,y:
CHAN OF INT ch1,ch2:
IF
  x = 1
    ch1! y
  x = 2
    ch2! y
  TRUE
    SKIP
```

In this example, "x" is tested. If it equals 1 or 2, "y" is output over either channel "ch1" or "ch2" respectively. If neither condition is true, the last condition is obviously TRUE and the SKIP process is executed. (Note that occam requires some sort of process following the condition).

IF, therefore, takes any number of processes and converts them into single processes to be executed. In the above example, had the last two lines been omitted and "x" had the value 3, say, then the resulting action would have been the equivalent of a STOP.

5.11 ALTERNATIVE PROCESSES

5.11.1 Alt Construct

ALT is an unfamiliar construct and is a common source of error in occam programming. Like IF, ALT converts a number of processes into a single process. Each of its constituent processes is headed by an input guard. Already described in Chapter 3.3.4, an ALT monitors each of its guards and executes the first guard to become ready - the choice being made in the **time** dimension.

Unlike IF, if no guard becomes ready, the ALT construct does not behave like STOP; instead it will **wait** until a guard becomes ready. Problems often arise as a result of this.

Both IF and ALT constructs can be nested.

5.11.2 Output Guards

It has already been noted in Chapter 3.3.4 that the use of output guards is not permitted in occam. For example, **the following code is impermissible:-**

```
INT x,y:
CHAN OF INT input,output:
WHILE TRUE
  ALT
    cond1 & output! x
      ... process 1
    input? y
      ... process 2
```

However, the following code **is permissible** and simulates the use of the output guard in the above code:-

```
INT x,y:
CHAN OF INT input,output:
WHILE TRUE
  ALT
    cond1 & SKIP
      output! x
      ...process 1
    input? y
      ...process 2
```

The third type of guard which may be used with an ALT construct is introduced here: **Boolean expression & SKIP**. Use of this guard enables "cond1" to be tested and, if TRUE, SKIP is executed and "x" is transmitted on channel "output", thereby simulating the behaviour of an output guard.

5.11.3 Prioritized ALT

In a standard ALT, if two guards become ready simultaneously, one of the corresponding two processes will be executed, the choice being arbitrary. (In a particular implementation of occam, this choice need not necessarily be **random**. However, the outcome of such a conflict is not defined by the language).

Occam provides a facility for prioritizing this choice by means of a PRI ALT construct. In the following example, it is used to properly terminate a WHILE loop:

```
BOOL running:
SEQ
  running := TRUE
  WHILE running
    INT x,y,any:
    CHAN OF INT ch1,ch2,exit:
    PRI ALT
      exit? any
        running:= FALSE
      ch1? x
        ... process 1
      ch2? y
        ... process 2
```

If a basic ALT construct had been used here, instead of a PRI ALT, we would have no guarantee that channel "exit" would ever be read and therefore that the loop would be completed.

It will be recognised that execution of the above code may result in data not being properly flushed out of channels "ch1" and "ch2". However this is a separate issue which we do not address here.

5.12 REPLICATORS

The replicator device, already introduced by means of examples in Chapter 4.3 and 4.4, is used together with a SEQ, PAR, ALT or IF construct to create an array of similar processes.

Using this device, the code below on the left, representing the Funnel example in Chapter 3.4.1, may be more succinctly written, resulting in the code below on the right:-

```
WHILE TRUE                      WHILE TRUE
  SEQ                             SEQ
    ALT                             ALT i = 0 FOR n
      in.1? data                      in[i]? data
        SKIP                            SKIP
      in.2? data                    ... process input data
        SKIP                        out! processed.data
        .
        .
        .
      in.n? data
        SKIP
    ... process input data
    out! processed.data
```

The general form of a replicator is:-

```
REP index = base FOR count
    ...process
```

where REP represents either SEQ, PAR, ALT or IF. It is not permitted to input or assign to the replicator index. Further, it is not possible to cause partial execution of a replicated construct.

Through the replicator construct we are now able to realize the second type of looping, described in Section 5.10 - repeat for a specified number of times. This can be accomplished using a replicated SEQ thus :-

```
SEQ i = 0 FOR n
    ... process
```

This is equivalent to the execution of "process" n times in sequence.

A replicated PAR statement can be used to effect to realise a pipeline structure (Chapter 3.4.2) :-

```
PAR i = 0 FOR 10
  SEQ
    ch[i]? data
    ... process i
    ch[i+1]! processed.data
```

This example assumes that is possible to represent the individual processes of the pipeline in a generalised process description. Ten parallel processes are created, each of which continually processes data received on the input channel, outputting the processed data on the output channel. Note that occam does not permit the count in a replicated PAR to be a variable, since the required number of processes must be set up at compile time. This restriction does not hold for replicated SEQ, ALT or IF constructs.

5.13 CONCURRENT PROGRAM TERMINATION

A new difficulty facing programmers, whose only experience is of sequential programming, is that of correct termination of concurrent programs. In a sequential program there is only one execution path. Irrespective of possible branching options, it is relatively straightforward for the programmer to arrange for this single path to be intercepted and execution terminated. Concurrent programs, however, may have many execution paths, which, if they are not terminated in the correct manner, may lead to deadlock situations.

We have already seen that the use of STOP will **not** terminate a process. Indeed, the use of STOP leads to loss of control over the process and, of course, in critical applications this may have alarming consequences.

Another possible solution method, which employs a global variable as a flag to signal termination to a set of parallel processes, is impermissible. Occam does not permit the use of shared variables between parallel processes. Instead, communication of termination information is made via channels.

The solution technique, adopted in the pipeline example below [3], is to flush out the pipeline by means of transmitting a termination flag over its channels. This flag is transmitted to each pipeline stage which passes it on to the next stage before terminating itself.

Consider again, the pipeline example, introduced in Chapter 3.4.2 and refined here in Section 5.12, now addressing the termination issue. The processes involved are :- "input", n "pipeline" processes and "output" (see Fig.5.5).

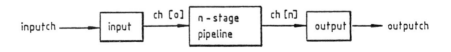

Fig.5.5 Pipeline example

The following code demonstrates the technique of flushing data through the processes to achieve satisfactory program termination:-

```
...declarations, definitions
...other processes
PROC input ()
  INT sample:
  BOOL running:
  SEQ
    running := TRUE
    WHILE running
      SEQ
        inputch? sample
        IF
          sample < 0
            SEQ
              ch[0]! sample
              running := FALSE
          sample >= 0
            ch[0]! sample
:
PROC pipeline ()
  PAR i = 0 FOR n
    INT data,processed.data:
    BOOL running:
    SEQ
      running := TRUE
      WHILE running
        SEQ
          ch[i]? data
          IF
            data < 0
              SEQ
                ch[i+1]! data
                running := false
            data >= 0
              SEQ
                ...process i
                ch[i+1]! processed.data
:
```

```
PROC output ()
  INT result:
  BOOL running:
  SEQ
    running := TRUE
    WHILE running
      SEQ
        ch[n]? result
        IF
          result < 0
            running := FALSE
          result >= 0
            outputch! result
:
PAR
  input ()
  pipeline ()
  output ()
```

In this example, we assume that the number of samples can only be determined at run time. The simple ploy of indicating end of data with a negative number is used. Each of the input and pipe stages identify receipt of this end-of-data flag, transmit it to the next stage and then terminate. All of the individual samples are thus processed through the system and transmitted to the output stage. Finally, the output stage receives and identifies the end-of-data flag and terminates.

5.14 MAPPING PROCESSES ONTO PROCESSORS

In a typical development procedure, an occam program may be tested and debugged on a single processor machine. The ultimate goal, however, is usually to map this program onto a fixed number of processors running in parallel. The number of **processors** need not necessarily match the number of designated **processes** and, in many cases, there will be more processes than processors.

Occam provides the means to allocate these abstract processes to the actual hardware processors by using PLACED PAR statements. Each PLACED PAR statement is followed by a placement statement allocating a specific processor for the execution of the process that follows.

It is also possible to allocate a named variable, channel, port or array to a physical memory address.

5.15 EXAMPLE PROGRAM

We close with a matrix multiplication example which illustrates and integrates many of the program elements described in this Chapter.

The program multiplies two 2*2 matrices, A and B, placing the resultant 2*2 matrix in C. This multiplication requires the following computation :-

$$C(i,j) = \quad A(i,k) * B(k,j) \quad i,j = 1,2.$$

The code is block-structured, consisting of the main procedure **matmult** followed by the main program. Procedure **matmult** has three procedures nested within it : **mult, add** and **calcelement**. The main program initialises matrices A and B, contains a simple instance of **matmult** and closes with an output handling sequence. The main procedure **matmult** calculates the individual elements, C(i,j), of the result matrix in parallel. Procedure **calcelement** itself calculates and sums the products A(i,k)*B(k,j) in parallel to generate each of the resultant matrix elements.

```
PROC matmult ( CHAN keyboard,screen) -- defines interface
                                     -- with PC.
  [2][2]REAL32 a,b,c :    --Define a,b,c to be 2*2 Matrices
  INT char :              -- For termination

-- COMMENT PROC REAL32write  writes a real number to
-- the screen

  PROC REAL32write (VAL REAL32 rX, VAL INT Ip, Dp)
  PROC matmult ( [][]REAL32 a,b,[][]REAL32 c)
    -- Process to multiply the matrices a and b together.
    -- returns answer in c.

    -- sizes of matrices are defined by
    -- rowsize (no. of rows) and colsize(no of cols)

  VAL rowsize1 IS 2 :
  VAL colsize1 IS 2 :
  VAL rowsize2 IS 2 :
  VAL colsize2 IS 2 :

  PROC mult ( CHAN result, VAL REAL32 a,b)
    REAL32 data :
    SEQ
      data:=a*b         --peform multiplication
      result ! data   --send result onto channel 'result'
  :
```

```
PROC add ( []CHAN in, CHAN out)
  INT count :
  REAL32 sum,x :
  SEQ
    count := 0
    sum:=0.0(REAL32)
    WHILE count < colsize1      -- continue until all
                                -- values have been
                                -- collected
        ALT i=0 FOR colsize1
          in[i] ? x             -- monitor 'in' channels
                                -- for data
              SEQ
                sum:=sum+x
                count:=count+1
      out ! sum                 -- after collecting all
:                               -- values, send result
                                -- element on channel 'out'

PROC calcelement( CHAN element, VAL INT i,j,
VAL [][]REAL32 a,b)
  [colsize1]CHAN out :
  PAR
    PAR k=0 FOR colsize1        -- defines the elements to
                                -- be multiplied
        mult(out[k],a[i][k],b[k][j])   -- calculate
                                -- products, send on
                                -- channel  'out'
    add(out,element)            -- read values from 'out'
                                -- channel,and send the
:                               -- sum  on channel 'element'
--
-- main body
--
[rowsize1][colsize2]CHAN element :
INT count :
SEQ
  count := 0
  PAR
    PAR i=0 FOR rowsize1
      PAR j=0 FOR colsize2
        calcelement(element[i][j],i,j,a,b)   --calculate
                                -- all the elements and send
                                -- to channel 'element'
    WHILE count < (rowsize1*colsize2) -- collect all
                                      -- elements
        ALT i=0 FOR rowsize1
          ALT j=0 FOR colsize2
            element[i][j] ? c[i][j]   -- read element
                                -- (from channel 'element')
                                -- and place in result matrix
                count:=count + 1
:
```

```
SEQ
-- initialise matrix A and output to screen
   SEQ i=0 FOR 2
      SEQ j=0 FOR 2
         a[i][j]:=1.0(REAL32)
   SEQ i=0 FOR 2
      SEQ
         REAL32write(a[i][0],0,0)
         screen ! tt.out.byte,' ',tt.out.byte,' '
         REAL32write(a[i][0],0,0)
         screen ! tt.out.byte,'*c',tt.out.byte,'*n'
   screen ! tt.out.byte,'*c',tt.out.byte,'*n'
-- initialise matrix B and output to screen
   SEQ i=0 FOR 2
      SEQ j=0 FOR 2
         b[i][j]:=2.0(REAL32)
   SEQ i=0 FOR 2
      SEQ
         REAL32write(b[i][0],0,0)
         screen ! tt.out.byte,' ',tt.out.byte,' '
         REAL32write(b[i][0],0,0)
         screen ! tt.out.byte,'*c',tt.out.byte,'*n'
   screen ! tt.out.byte,'*c',tt.out.byte,'*n'
   matmult(a,b,c)
-- output result matrix C to screen
   SEQ i=0 FOR 2
      SEQ
         REAL32write(c[i][0],0,0)
         screen ! tt.out.byte,' ',tt.out.byte,' '
         REAL32write(c[i][0],0,0)
         screen ! tt.out.byte,'*c',tt.out.byte,'*n'
   screen ! tt.out.byte,'*c',tt.out.byte,'*n'
-- Program terminates after a key press
   keyboard ? char
:
```

This example also serves to illustrate the possible complexity arising out of parallel algorithm development compared with its sequential equivalent :-

```
begin
   for i := 1 to index1 do
      for j := 1 to index2 do
         begin
            temp := 0.0;
            for k:= 1 to index3 do
               temp := temp + a(i,k)*b(k,j);
            c(i,j) := temp;
         end;
   end;
```

ACKNOWLEDGEMENTS

Special thanks are due to P. Entwistle, D. Lawrie and F. Garcia (members of the Bangor Control Software Group), who have all contributed in a variety of ways to the final version of this Chapter.   David Lawrie contributed the Example Program given in Section 5.15.

REFERENCES

1. "Occam Programming Manual", 1984, INMOS Ltd, Prentice Hall.

2. May, D., "Occam 2 Language Definition", INMOS Ltd.

3. Pountain, D., 1988, "A Tutorial Introduction to OCCAM Programming", Blackwell.

Chapter 6

The transputer implementation of occam

David May and Roger Shepherd of INMOS Limited
©INMOS Limited 1987. Reproduced by kind permission of Prentice Hall

6.1 INTRODUCTION

VLSI technology allows a large number of identical devices to be manufactured cheaply. For this reason, it is attractive to implement an occam [1] program using a number of identical components, each programmed with the appropriate occam[1] process. A transputer [2] is such a component.

A transputer is a single VLSI device with memory, processor and communications links for direct connection to other transputers. Concurrent systems can be constructed from a collection of transputers which operate concurrently and communicate through links.

The transputer can therefore be used as a building block for concurrent processing systems, with occam as the associated design formalism.

6.2 ARCHITECTURE

An important property of VLSI technology is that communication between devices is very much slower than communication on the same device. In a computer, almost every operation that the processor performs involves the use of memory. A transputer therefore includes both processor and memory in the same integrated circuit device.

In any system constructed from integrated circuit devices, much of the physical bulk arises from connections between devices. The size of the package for an integrated circuit is determined more by the number of connection pins than by the size of the device itself. In addition, connections between devices provided by paths on a circuit board consume a considerable amount of space.

---

[1]occam is a trademark of the INMOS Group of Companies

The speed of communication between electronic devices is optimised by the use of uni-directional signal wires, each connecting two devices. If any devices are connected by a shared bus, electrical problems of driving the bus require that the speed is reduced. Also, additional control logic and wiring is required to control sharing of the bus.

To provide maximum speed with minimal wiring, the transputer uses point-to-point serial communication links for direct connection to other transputers.

6.3 THE TRANSPUTER

A transputer system consists of a number of interconnected transputers, each executing an occam process and communicating with other transputers. As a process executed by a transputer may itself consist of a number of concurrent processes the transputer has to support the occam programming model internally. Within a transputer concurrent processing is implemented by sharing the processor time between the concurrent processes.

The most effective implementation of simple programs by a programmable computer is provided by a sequential processor. Consequently, the transputer processor is fairly conventional, except that additional hardware and microcode support the occam model of concurrent processing.

6.3.1 Sequential Processing

The design of the transputer processor exploits the availability of fast on-chip memory by having only a small number of registers; six registers are used in the execution of a sequential process. The small number of registers, together with the simplicity of the instruction set enables the processor to have relatively simple (and fast) data-paths and control logic.

The six registers (see Fig.6.1) are:

The workspace pointer which points to an area of store where local variables are kept.

The instruction pointer which points to the next instruction to be executed.

The operand register which is used in the formation of instruction operands.

The A, B and C registers which form an evaluation stack, and are the sources and destinations for most arithmetic and logical operations. Loading a value into the stack pushes B into C, and A into B, before loading A. Storing a value from A, pops B into A and C into B.

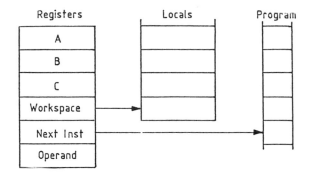

Fig.6.1 Registers

Expressions are evaluated on the evaluation stack, and instructions refer to the stack implicitly. For example, the 'add' instruction adds the top two values in the stack and places the result on the top of the stack. The use of a stack removes the need for instructions to respecify the location of their operands. Statistics gathered from a large number of programs show that three registers provide an effective balance between code compactness and implementation complexity.

No hardware mechanism is provided to detect that more than three values have been loaded onto the stack. it is easy for the compiler to ensure that this never happens.

6.3.2 Instructions

It was a design decision that the transputer should be programmed in a high-level language. The instruction set has, therefore, been designed for simple and efficient compilation. It contains a relatively small number of instructions, all with the same format, chosen to give a compact representation of the operations most frequently occurring in programs. The instruction set is independent of the processor wordlength, allowing the same microcode to be used for transputers with different wordlengths. Each instruction consists of a single byte divided into two 4 bit parts. The four most significant bits of the byte are a function code, and the four least significant bits are a data value.

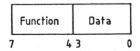

Fig.6.2 Instruction format

6.3.2.1 Direct functions

The representation provides for sixteen functions, each with a data value ranging from 0 to 15. Thirteen of these are used to encode the most important functions performed by any computer. These include:

load constant
add constant

load local
store local
load local pointer

load non-local
store non-local

jump
conditional jump

call

The most common operations in a program are the loading of small literal values, and the loading and storing of one of a small number of variables. The 'load constant' instruction enables values between 0 and 15 to be loaded with a single byte instruction. The 'load local' and 'store local' instructions access locations in memory relative to the workspace pointer. The first 16 locations can be accessed using a single byte instruction.

The 'load non-local' and 'store non-local' instructions behave similarly, except that they access locations in memory relative to the A register. Compact sequences of these instructions allow efficient access to data structures, and provide for simple implementations of the static links or displays used in the implementation of block structured programming languages such as occam.

6.3.2.2 Prefix functions

Two more of the function codes are used to allow the operand of any instruction to be extended in length. These are:

prefix
negative prefix

All instructions are executed by loading the four data bits into the least significant four bits of the operand register, which is then used as the instruction's operand. All instructions except the prefix instructions end by clearing the operand register, ready for the next instruction.

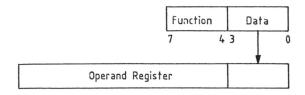

Fig.6.3 Loading of data bits into the operand register

The 'prefix' instruction loads its four data bits into the operand register, and then shifts the operand register up four places. The 'negative prefix' instruction is similar, except that it complements the operand register before shifting it up. Consequently, operands can be extended to any length up to the length of the operand register by a sequence of prefix instructions. In particular, operands in the range -256 to 255 can be represented using one prefix instruction.

The use of prefix instructions has certain beneficial consequences. Firstly, they are decoded and executed in the same way as every other instruction, which simplifies and speeds instruction decoding. Secondly, they simplify language compilation, by providing a completely uniform way of allowing any instruction to take an operand of any size. Thirdly, they allow operands to be represented in a form independent of the processor wordlength.

6.3.2.3 Indirect functions

The remaining function code, 'operate', causes its operand to be interpreted as an operation on the values held in the evaluation stack. This allows up to 16 such operations to be encoded in a single byte instruction. However, the prefix instructions can be used to extend the operand of an 'operate' instruction just like any other. The instruction representation therefore provides for an infinite number of operations.

The encoding of the indirect functions is chosen so that the most frequently occurring operations are represented without the use of a prefix instruction. These include arithmetic, logical and comparison operations such as:

add
exclusive or
greater than.

Less frequently occurring operations have encodings which require a single prefix operation (the transputer instruction set is not large enough to require more than 512 operations to be encoded!).

6.3.3 Expression Evaluation

Evaluation of expressions may require the use of temporary variables in the process workspace, but the number of these can be minimised by careful choice of the evaluation order.

Let **depth(e)** be the number of stack locations needed for the evaluation of expression **e**, defined by:

```
depth(constant) = 1
depth(variable) = 1
depth(e1 op e2) = IF depth(e1) > depth(e2) THEN
                       depth(e1)
                  ELSE IF depth(e1) < depth(e2) THEN
                       depth(e2)
                  ELSE depth(e1) + 1
```

Let **commutes(operator)** be **true** if the operator commutes, **false** otherwise.

Let **e1** and **e2** be expressions. The expression of **(e1 op e2)** is compiled for the 3 register stack by:

```
compile(e1 op e2)=
  IF depth(e2) > depth(e1)
  THEN
    IF depth(e1) > 2
    THEN (compile(e2);store temp;compile(e1);load temp; op
    ELSE IF commutes(op)
       THEN (compile(e2);compile(e1);op)
       ELSE (compile(e2);compile(e1);reverse;op)
  ELSE
    IF depth(e2) < 3
    THEN (compile(e1);compile(e2);op)
    ELSE (compile(e2);store temp;compile(e1);load temp;op)
```

where (11;12; ... ln) represents instructions.

6.3.3.1 Efficiency of encoding

Measurements show that about 80% of executed instructions are encoded in a single byte (ie without the use of prefix instructions). Many of these instructions, such as 'load constant' and 'add' require just one processor cycle.

The instruction representation gives a more compact representation of high level language programs than more conventional instruction sets. Since a program requires less store to represent it, less of the memory bandwidth is taken up with fetching instructions. Furthermore, as memory is word accessed, the processor will receive several instructions for every fetch.

Short instructions also improve the effectiveness of instruction prefetch, which in turn improves processor performance. There is an extra word of prefetch buffer so that the processor rarely has to wait for an instruction fetch before proceeding. Since the buffer is short, there is little time penalty when a jump instruction causes the buffer contents to be discarded.

6.3.4 Support for Concurrency

The processor provides efficient support for the occam model of concurrency and communication. It has a microcoded scheduler which enables any number of concurrent processes to be executed together, sharing the processor time. This removes the need for a software kernel. The processor does not need to support the dynamic allocation of storage as the occam compiler is able to perform the allocation of space to concurrent processes.

At any time, a concurrent process may be:

active   -being executed
           -on a list waiting to be executed
inactive -ready to input
           -ready to output
           -waiting until a specified time

The scheduler operates in such a way that inactive processes do not consume any processor time.

The active processes waiting to be executed are held on a list. This is a linked list of process workspaces, implemented using two registers, one of which points to the first process on the list, the other to the last.

In Fig.6.4, S is executing, and P, Q and R are active, awaiting execution.

A process is executed until it is unable to proceed because it is waiting to input or output, or waiting for the timer. Whenever a process is unable to proceed, its instruction pointer is saved in its workspace and the next process is taken from the list. Actual process switch times are very small as little state needs to be saved; it is not necessary to save the evaluation stack on rescheduling.

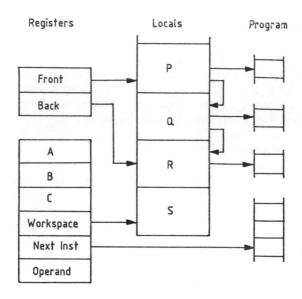

Fig.6.4 Implementation of scheduling

The processor provides a number of special operations to support the process model. These include

start process
end process

When a parallel construct is executed, 'start process' instructions are used to create the necessary concurrent processes. A 'start process' instruction creates a new process by adding a new workspace to the end of the scheduling list, enabling the new concurrent process to be executed together with the ones already being executed.

The correct termination of a parallel construct is assured by use of the 'end process' instruction. This uses a workspace location as a counter of the components of the parallel construct which have still to terminate. The counter is initialised to the number of components before the processes are 'started'. Each component ends with an 'end process' instruction which decrements and tests the counter. For all but the last component, the counter is non-zero and the component is descheduled. For the last component, the counter is zero and the component continues.

6.3.4.1 Communications

As we have already seen in Chapter 3, communication between processes is achieved by means of channels. Occam communication is point-to-point, synchronised and unbuffered. As a result, a channel needs no process queue, no message queue and no message buffer.

A channel between two processes executing on the same transputer is implemented by a single word in memory; a channel between processes executing on different transputers is implemented by point-to-point links. The processor provides a number of operations to support message passing, the most important being:

> input message
> output message

The 'input message' and 'output message' instruction use the address of the channel to determine whether the channel is internal or external. This means that the same instruction sequence can be used for both hard and soft channels, allowing a process to be written and compiled without knowledge of where its channels are connected.

As in the occam model, communication takes place when both the inputting and outputting processes are ready. Consequently, the process which first becomes ready must wait until the second one is also ready.

A process performs an input or output by loading the evaluation stack with a pointer to a message, the address of a channel, and a count of the number of bytes to be transferred, and then executing an 'input message' or an 'output message' instruction.

6.3.4.2 Internal channel communication

At any time, an internal channel (a single word in memory) either holds the identity of a process, or holds the special value 'empty'. The channel is initialised to 'empty' before it is used.

When a message is passed using the channel, the identity of the first process to become ready is stored in the channel, and the processor starts to execute the next process from the scheduling list. When the second process to use the channel becomes ready, the message is copied, the waiting process is added to the scheduling list, and the channel reset to its initial state. It does not matter whether the inputting or the outputting process becomes ready first.

In the Fig.6.5a, a process P is about to execute an output instruction on an 'empty' channel C. The evaluation stack holds a pointer to a message, the address of channel C, and a count of the number of bytes in the message.

After executing the output instruction (Fig.6.5b), the channel C holds the address of the workspace of P, and the address of the message to be transferred is stored in the workspace of P. P is descheduled, and the process starts to execute the next process from the scheduling list.

The channel C and process P remain in this state until a second process, Q, (Fig.6.5c) executes an output instruction on the channel.

The message is copied, the waiting process P is added to the scheduling list, and the channel C is reset to its initial 'empty' state (Fig.6.5d).

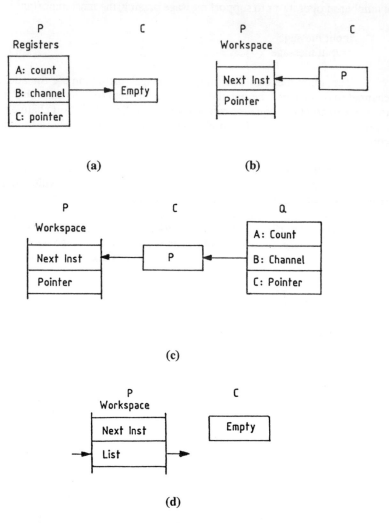

Fig.6.5 Internal channel communication mechanism

6.3.3.3 External channel communication

When a message is passed via an external channel, the processor delegates to an autonomous link interface the job of transferring the message and deschedules the process. When the message has been transferred, the link interface causes the processor to reschedule the waiting process. This allows the processor to continue the execution of other processes whilst the external message transfer is taking place.

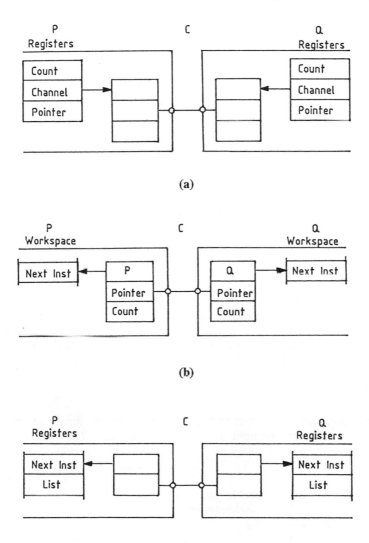

(a)

(b)

(c)

Fig.6.6 External channel communication mechanism

Each link interface uses three registers:

a pointer to a process workspace
a pointer to a message
a count of bytes in the message.

In Fig.6.6a, processes P and Q, executed by different transputers, communicate using a channel C implemented by a link connecting two transputers. P outputs, and Q inputs.

When P executes its instruction, the registers in the link interface of the transputer executing P are initialised, and P is descheduled. Similarly, when Q executes its input instruction, the registers in the link interface of the process executing Q are initialised, and Q is descheduled (see Fig.6.6b).

The message is now copied through the link, after which the workspaces of P and Q are returned to the corresponding scheduling lists (Fig.6.6c). The protocol used on P and Q ensures that it does not matter which of P and Q first becomes ready.

6.3.4.4 Timer

The transputer has a clock which 'ticks' every microsecond. The current value of the processor clock can be ready by executing a 'Read timer' instruction.

A process can arrange to perform a 'timer input', in which case it will become ready to execute after a specified time has been reached.

The timer input instruction requires a time to be specified. If this time is in the 'past' (i.e. ClockReg AFTER SpecifiedTime) then the instruction has no effect. If the time is in the 'future' (i.e. SpecifiedTime AFTER ClockReg or SpecifiedTime = ClockReg) then the process is descheduled. When the specified time is reached the process is scheduled again.

6.3.4.5 ALT construct

The occam ALT construct enables a process to wait for input from any one of a number of channels, or until a specific time occurs. This requires special instructions, as the normal 'input' instruction deschedules a process until a specific channel becomes ready, or until a specific time is reached. The instructions used are:

enable channel   enable timer
disable channel   disable timer
alternative wait.

The ALT construct is implemented by 'enabling' the channel input or time input specified in each of its components. The 'alternative wait' is then used to deschedule the process if none of the channel or timer inputs is ready; the process will be re-scheduled when any one of them becomes ready. The channel and timer inputs are then 'disabled'. The 'disable' instructions are also designed to select the component of the alternative to be executed; the first component found to be ready is executed.

6.3.5 Inter-transputer Links

To provide synchronised communication, each message must be acknowledged. Consequently, a link requires at least one signal wire in each direction.

A link between two transputers is implemented by connecting a link interface on one transputer to a link interface on the other transputer by two one-directional signal lines, along which data is transmitted serially.

The two signal wires of the link can be used to provide two occam channels, one in each direction. This requires a simple protocol. Each signal line carries data and control information.

The link protocol provides the synchronised communication of occam. The use of a protocol providing for the transmission of any arbitrary sequence of bytes allows transputers of different wordlength to be connected.

Each message is transmitted as a sequence of single byte communications, requiring only the presence of a single byte buffer in the receiving transputer to ensure that no information is lost. Each byte is transmitted as a start bit followed by a one bit followed by the eight data bits followed by a stop bit. After transmitting a data byte, the sender waits until an acknowledge is received; this consists of a start bit followed by a zero bit. The acknowledge signifies both that a process was able to receive the acknowledged byte, and that the receiving link is able to receive another byte. The sending link reschedules the sending process only after the acknowledge for the final byte of the message has been received.

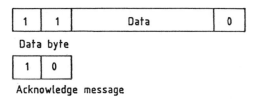

Data byte

Acknowledge message

Fig.6.7 Inter-transputer link protocol

Data bytes and acknowledges are multiplexed down each signal line. An acknowledge is transmitted as soon as reception of a data byte starts (if there is room to buffer another one). Consequently, transmission may be continuous, with no delays between data bytes.

6.4 SUMMARY

Experience with occam has shown that many applications naturally decompose into a large number of fairly simple processes. Once an application has been described in occam, a variety of implementations are possible. In particular, the use of occam together with the transputer enables the designer to exploit the performance and economics of VLSI technology. The concurrent processing features of occam can be efficiently implemented by a small, simple and fast processor.

The transputer therefore has two important uses. Firstly, it provides a new system 'building block' which enables occam to be used as a design formalism. In this role, occam serves both as a system description language and a programming language. Secondly, occam and the transputer can be used for prototyping highly concurrent systems in which the individual processes are ultimately intended to be implemented by dedicated hardware.

REFERENCES

1. Occam Programming Manual, 1984, Prentice-Hall International.

2. IMS T414 reference manual, 1985, Inmos Limited.

Transputer applications

A variety of control applications of Transputer-based systems is described and the advantages and disadvantages of using the Transputer for these examples are revealed. Performance results are included to provide quantitative measures of the potential improvements likely to be realised through the application of parallel processing systems.

Field-oriented control of a.c. induction motors is the subject of two studies. In the first, it is demonstrated that by decoupling the torque and field current components of the machine and implementing vector control as three parallel processes, the new strategy compares favourably with previous vector control systems. A user interactive open-loop controller for the induction motor drive is developed in the second study. This is achieved using a single Transputer for the real-time generation of pulse width modulated waveforms, indicating the potential for the development of an induction motor drive rig with considerable real-time processing ability through the introduction of additional processors.

Two case studies, flight control and robotics, employ static and dynamic load-balancing methods to distribute the computing burden evenly over the parallel processing system. The results of these studies reveal the strengths and shortcomings of each approach. In the last application example, the suitability of the Group Method of Data Handling for the parallel implementation of an identification algorithm is exploited on a 4-Transputer system resulting in a speedup factor of 2 over a single Transputer arrangement. Its application as a decision-maker in medical diagnosis is demonstrated.

Issues relating to the design of fault-tolerant concurrent software are explored in some depth. Software fault-tolerance procedures for both sequential and parallel real-time systems are described. It is shown that techniques such as recovery blocks, conversation schemes and concurrent watchdog mechanisms can be used to protect specific processes and functions and can also be used to protect interprocess communications to safeguard synchronisation and the satisfactory operation of concurrent systems. Occam examples are used to illustrate the methods.

Chapter 7

Control applications of transputers

Dr. D.I. Jones & Dr. P.J. Fleming

7.1 INTRODUCTION

In this Chapter, we discuss the use of parallel processing techniques in real-time control with particular reference to the INMOS transputer and its associated programming language, occam.

We describe the occam structures that are applicable to three particular applications in control engineering:

(a) Field oriented control of a.c. induction motors,

(b) Development of a multiprocessor-based flight controller, and

(c) Calculation of the inverse dynamics equations for robots.

7.2 FIELD ORIENTED (VECTOR) CONTROL OF A.C.INDUCTIONMOTORS

In this Section, we describe a study, conducted in collaboration with the University of Nottingham, which establishes how transputers may be used to implement a field-oriented controller.

The a.c.induction motor, incorporating field oriented control, is presently one of the prime candidates as a substitute for d.c. machines in variable speed drives. The aim of this technique is to decouple the torque and field current components of the machine so that it may be controlled in the same manner as a d.c. machine, leading to an improved transient response [1].

A d.c. machine, as illustrated in Fig.7.1, is controlled by means of two separate currents. The field current (i_{ds}) controls the gap flux (ψ_{dr}), whereas the torque (T) is controlled by the armature current (i_{qs}), such that:

$$\psi\, dr = L_m\, i_{ds}$$

(7.1)

$$T = K_t\, \psi_{dr}\, i_{qs},$$

(7.2)

where K_t and L_m are machine constants and the notation is chosen to be consistent with that of a.c.machines.

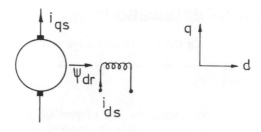

Fig.7.1 The d.c. machine

It is usual to keep the gap flux at a constant value just under saturation on the machine's magnetisation curve. Thereafter, the torque is varied by means of the armature current, usually in a feedback loop to keep rotor speed constant in the face of varying load. The important point is that **independent** control of field flux and torque is possible. It is the switching action of the commutator, maintaining the field and rotor fluxes at right angles, which decouples the two components.

The a.c. induction machine has no commutator and the corresponding equations are more complex. Expressed in a dq reference frame the equations for gap flux and torque are as follows [1]:

$$\psi_{dr} = L_m\, i_{ds} + L_r\, i_{qr}$$

(7.3)

$$T = (3/2)\, P\, (L_m/L_r)\, [\psi_{dr}\, i_{qs} - L_m\, i_{qs}\, i_{ds} - L_r\, i_{ds}\, i_{qr}]$$

(7.4)

where

L_m, L_r are motor inductance parameters,
ψ_{qr}, ψ_{dr} are quadrature and direct components of rotor flux,
i_{qr}, i_{dr} are quadrature and direct components of rotor current,
i_{qs}, i_{ds} are quadrature and direct components of stator current, and
P is the number of poles on the machine.

Comparing equations (7.1) and (7.3) and (7.2) and (7.4), respectively, shows that there are additional terms in the a.c. machine equations. It is the goal of vector control to eliminate these terms and achieve decoupled control of torque and gap flux.

An outline of the field-oriented control system is shown in Fig.7.2.

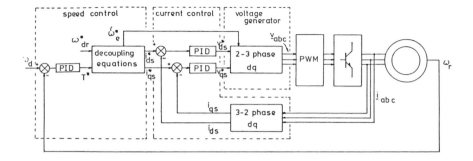

Fig.7.2 Block diagram of field oriented control system

It is divided into three parts:

(a) voltage generation,
(b) current transformation and control,
(c) decoupling computation and speed control.

It may be shown, [1], that non-interacting control is achieved by defining the following set of conditions on the armature currents and inverter frequency which the controller must always satisfy:

$$i^*{}_{qs} = (2/3P)\ (L_r/L_m)\ (T^*/\psi^*{}_{dr}),$$
(7.5)

$$i^*{}_{ds} = (1/L_m)\ \psi^*{}_{dr},$$
(7.6)

$$\omega_e = (2/3P)\ R_r\ [T^*/(\psi^*{}_{dr})^2 + \omega_r],$$
(7.7)

where R_r is the rotor resistance,
ω_e is the inverter frequency, and
ω_r is the rotor measured angular speed.

The asterisk notation is used to emphasise that the torque and gap flux are demanded values (supplied by the speed control loop).

The speed control section must compute these decoupling equations as well as the normal PID compensation.

Referring to Fig.7.2, we see that the computed values of i^*_{qs} and i^*_{ds} are then used as demanded values to the current control section. They form error signals with the measured values of i_{qs} and i_{ds} which are dynamically compensated to form the desired motor voltages v^*_{qs} and v^*_{ds}.

In turn v^*_{qs} and v^*_{ds} are the inputs to the voltage generator section. The actual 3-phase a.c. voltages v_{abc}, required by the machine windings, are given by the transformation

$$\begin{bmatrix} v_{as} \\ v_{bs} \\ v_{cs} \end{bmatrix} = \begin{bmatrix} \cos \omega_e t & \sin \omega_e t & 0 \\ \cos(\omega_e t - 2\pi/3) & \sin(\omega_e t - 2\pi/3) & 0 \\ \cos(\omega_e t + 2\pi/3) & \sin(\omega_e t + 2\pi/3) & 0 \end{bmatrix} \begin{bmatrix} v^*_{qs} \\ v^*_{ds} \\ 0 \end{bmatrix} \quad (7.8)$$

Similarly, the measured currents i_{abc} must be transformed into the dq reference frame to form i_{qs} and i_{ds}, by the transpose of the matrix equation (7.8).

7.2.1 Implementation

The occam implementation of this system is written as three parallel processes:

```
PAR
    voltage.generator  (    )
    current.control    (    )
    speed.control      (    )
```

The mainstream of dataflow is governed by "current.control", the pseudo-code for which is given below.

```
PROC current.control (  ) =
WHILE TRUE
  ALT
    demand.current? i*ds       -- update current
      demand.current ?  i*qs   -- demand (slow)
    fast.clock ? ANY
      SEQ
        ADC ? iabc                   -- measure currents
        cc.to.table ! ANY                   --access curren
        table.to.cc ? sin ωet ; cos ωet ... --table values
        ... dq and 3 --> 2 transform obtains ids and iqs
        ... error and PID obtains v*ds and v*qs
        ... dq, 2 --> 3 transform obtains vabc
        output.voltages ! vas ; vbs ; vcs  :
```

The first part of the ALT construct allows the demanded currents to be updated at a relatively slow rate without affecting the flow of current control. The second part of the ALT runs at the sample rate of the current loop. In the transputer-based PWM waveform generator, being developed at Nottingham University, the carrier is set at 2kHz and each current is sampled twice per period. This allows 250µs of computation time before the next sample. Within this time the currents must be measured, the input transformation, PID compensation and the output transformation performed and v_{abc} output.

Pseudo-code for "speed.control" is given below. This is governed by a relatively slow real-time clock. It is a simple sequential loop involving speed measurement (ω_r), calculation of the decoupling equations (7.5-7.7) and communication of i^*_{qs} and i^*_{ds} to "current.control" and ω_e to process "voltage.generator".

```
PROC speed.control ( ) =
WHILE TRUE
  SEQ
    slow.clock ? ANY
    ... measure rotor speed ωr
    ... calculate  i*ds, i*qs, ωe
    input.freq ! ωe    -- send inverter frequency
    demand.current ! i*ds ; i*qs  : -- send demand current
```

Process "voltage.generator" is in fact two parallel processes as shown in the structure diagram, Fig.7.3, and in the pseudo-code which follows the Figure.

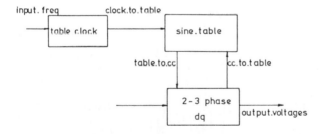

Fig.7.3 Structure of "voltage.generator"

```
PROC voltage.generator ( ) =
WHILE TRUE
  PAR
    table.clock (clock.to.table, input.freq)
    sine.table (clock.to.table, table.to.cc, cc.to.table)
```

The "table.clock" and "sine.table" procedures are as follows:

```
PROC table.clock ( ) =
WHILE TRUE
  ALT
    input.freq ? ωe -- get inverter frequency
      interval := 1/(N * ωe)    -- timer interval
    TIME ? AFTER (next.time)
      SEQ
        clock.to.table ! ANY  -- signal to increment table
        next.time := next.time + interval  :

PROC sine.table ( ) =
WHILE TRUE
  ALT
    clock.to.table ? ANY
    ... increment table pointers
    cc.to.table ? ANY
    ... access sin ωet, cos ωet ...
    table.to.cc ! sin ωet, cos ωet    :
```

The generation of the $\cos(\omega_e t)$ and $\sin(\omega_e t)$ terms necessary for equation (7.8) is accomplished by a driven sine-table. The real-time clock is used to step a pointer through a modulo-N sine table at a rate determined by ω_e (typically 20-100 Hz), the required inverter frequency. Cosine values are given by another pointer N/4 elements displaced in the table while supply phases b and c are given by the elements N/3, respectively, displaced from phase a.

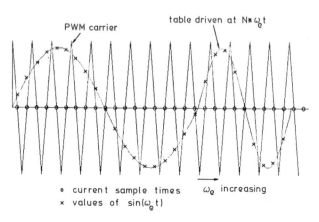

o   current sample times ω_e increasing
x   values of $\sin(\omega_e t)$

Fig.7.4 Relationship between carrier and modulating sinewave

Process "current.control" interrogates the state of this table, at each sample time. Thus, "voltage.generator" effectively provides modulating sine/cosine waveforms at a frequency ω_e, which are changed in phase and amplitude by the output transform to give the 3 phase a.c. output, v_{abc}. This is illustrated in Fig.7.4.

7.2.2 Performance

The voltage generator process has been implemented on a Stride workstation using occam1 and downloading to a B001 board. For a 96 point sinetable and 32-bit integer arithmetic, the minimum computational time was found to be 50μs - a maximum 3-phase frequency of 200Hz. Output was to an 8-bit DAC via a link adapter and typical results are shown in Fig.7.5.

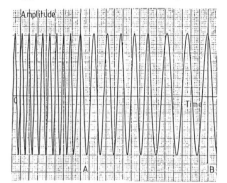 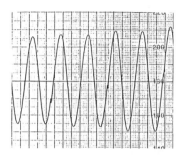

Fig.7.5 Typical output showing changes of frequency and amplitude

These traces imply that, even at 200Hz, we have 200μs left for the current control loop. We are currently developing an 8-channel, 12-bit ADC board using a link adapter and the prototype has demonstrated a read time for 3 channels of approximately 40μs. This leaves 160μs for the input transform and dynamic compensator which, we estimate, is just possible. Altogether, this implementation promises favourable comparison - in terms of software and hardware - with previous vector control systems [2].

The speed control loop must be implemented on a second transputer, which is not time-critical since the sampling rate may be relatively slow. However, if we recall equations (7.5) - (7.7), we see that complete decoupling depends entirely on a knowledge of the motor parameters. The change with machine operating condition of inductance parameters, L_r and L_m, is relatively small. However the rotor resistance (R_r) is sensitive to machine loading because of temperature variation. It is likely that the outer control loop must also perform some on-line identification of this parameter [1].

7.3 DIGITAL FLIGHT CONTROL

Complex digital controllers, such as those required for present and future aircraft, demand a powerful computing capability to achieve the required performance. Surveys have shown that parallel processing is a suitable vehicle for providing this facility.

This Section describes software and hardware aspects of a pilot study, undertaken in collaboration with Royal Aircraft Establishment, Bedford, to map an existing aircraft flight control law, the Versatile Auto-Pilot (VAP), onto a parallel processing system, investigating the potential of the transputer and occam, for the implementation of this control law.

The VAP control law was chosen because it is representative of a class of flight control laws. However, it is not particularly demanding for implementation on a "fast" transputer array. Its purpose, here, is to serve as a "Demonstrator" vehicle.

The VAP control law operates in three different modes: Height hold, Glidepath hold and Flare, depending on flight conditions , Goddard and Cooke [3]. Here we describe methods used to generate the concurrent realization for only one of these modes - the most complex - the Height hold mode shown in Fig.7.6, using two alternative mapping approaches: Parallel Branches and Heuristic. Both approaches are evaluated with respect to execution speed, ease of programming, adaptability and extendability.

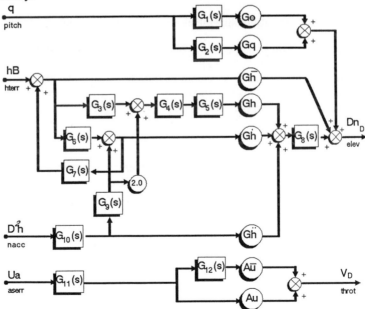

Fig 7.6 VAP Control law block schematic (Height hold mode)

7.3.1 VAP Control Law Software

7.3.1.1 Parallel branches approach

For this approach, the control law was modified, using block diagram transformations into a parallel network of transfer functions. Then, each of these parallel paths, in the new schematic block, was expanded into partial fractions and discretised to reduce the control law to a sum of simple discrete functions (e.g integrator, gain, first-order lag etc.), representing the software building blocks. The method used to discretise the resulting functions was the Pole-Zero mapping method. This method has been modified for computing the discrete equivalent function, adding one delay in response to the unit step input. The purpose of this is to allow one sample period in which to perform the calculation. Using this method the problem was broken down into 37 simple difference equations (see Fig.7.7).

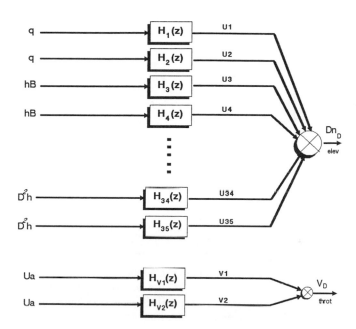

Fig. 7.7 VAP Control Law: Parallel Branches network (simplified representation)

These are then combined to form the control signals

$$Dn(k) = U1(k) + U2(k) + U3(k) + ... + U35(k)$$
$$VD(k) = V1(k) + V2(k),$$

where Dn and VD are the elevator and throttle demands and U1-U35 and V1,V2 are the results of the difference equations.

These equations were programmed as individual occam processes and then mapped into four larger processes T0 - T3 as shown in Fig.7.8.

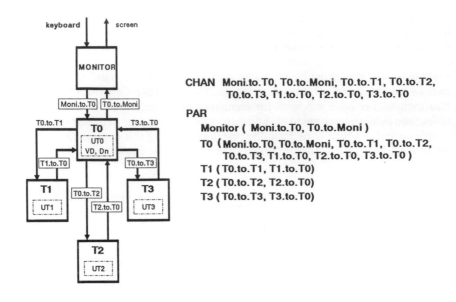

CHAN Moni.to.T0, T0.to.Moni, T0.to.T1, T0.to.T2,
          T0.to.T3, T1.to.T0, T2.to.T0, T3.to.T0

PAR

   Monitor (Moni.to.T0, T0.to.Moni)

   T0 (Moni.to.T0, T0.to.Moni, T0.to.T1, T0.to.T2,
           T0.to.T3, T1.to.T0, T2.to.T0, T3.to.T0)

   T1 (T0.to.T1, T1.to.T0)

   T2 (T0.to.T2, T2.to.T0)

   T3 (T0.to.T3, T3.to.T0)

**Fig 7.8 Occam Structure for VAP Control law using the Parallel
Branches Design Approach**

In the program, the process T0 inputs data from the Monitor process, which controls input and output. T0 then sends this data simultaneously to the T1, T2 and T3 processes. T0 evaluates VD (throttle demand) and UT0. Concurrently with this process, T1, T2 and T3 are executed. UT1, UT2 and UT3 are calculated and sent to T0, which evaluates Dn as a sum of UT0, UT1, UT2 and UT3. Finally, Dn and VD are broadcast over the T0.to.Moni channel to the Monitor process. These processes are repeated over each sample interval.In this case we assume that the sample interval begins when process Monitor receives all data values from an input channel (keyboard or link adaptor) and finishes when the Monitor sends the values Dn and VD to an output channel (screen or link adaptor).

The performance of this approach for different numbers of processors, (transputers), has been determined using the timing provided in occam by TIMER. A high priority timer process was included in the programs to provide a clock, "counting" every 1.0 microsecond, which is used to calculate the execution time and the average (%) transputer activity. The latter is the proportion of the total time for which any processor is usefully executing (not idling) and is a measure of system efficiency. The program was run on an IMS BOO3 evaluation board in conjunction with an IBM- PC and the results are shown in Table 7.1.

This Table shows a set of results obtained in the various configurations used, all from solving the same problem. The first set of results correspond to the allocation of all the processes on one transputer, which, obviously, spends all its time processing the control law. The second, third and fourth sets of results are obtained by mapping the processes onto two, three and four processors, respectively, showing a significant improvement in the execution time in comparison with the first set. However, at the same time, a deterioration in the processor average activity can be observed.

In general, in a multi-transputer configuration, one transputer will usually spend more time processing its given task than the others, even if the load has been balanced. This time, together with communications time, gives the total execution time taken by the network.

VAP CONTROL LAW : PARALLEL BRANCHES APPROACH

Execution time for 1 transputer : 2.762 ms

Transputer	Processor Activity	Average Activity
1	100%	100 %

Execution time for 2 transputers: 1.511 ms

Transputer	Processor Activity	Average Activity
1	100%	91%
2	82%	

Execution time for 3 transputers: 1.016 ms

Transputer	Processor Activity	Average Activity
1	100%	90%
2	85%	
3	85%	

Execution time for 4 transputers: 0.802 ms

Transputer	Processor Activity	Average Activity
1	94%	85%
2	84%	
3	81%	
4	81%	

Table 7.1 Performance of the Parallel Branches design approach

7.3.1.2 Heuristic approach

For the Heuristic approach, the VAP control law is considered in its original representation as shown in Fig.7.6, and the discrete equivalent of each transfer function block is calculated. Even though this structure consists of a collection of sequential blocks, through a reasoning process, parallelism in the structure is extracted through inspection of the paths' dependencies and non-dependencies.

The method used to discretise each block of the original control law diagram in this approach was again Pole-Zero mapping. However, the modified Pole-Zero mapping version was only used to discretise the transfer function blocks that are dependent on the control law inputs. Subsequent blocks were discretised using the original version of the method, where the outputs of the discrete-time equations require inputs at the same time, e(k).

Using this method, the outputs of the control law were reduced to the following sequence of computations:

$$Dn(k) = Dn0(k) + Dn1(k) + Dn2(k)$$
$$VD(k) = VD1(k) + VD2(k)$$

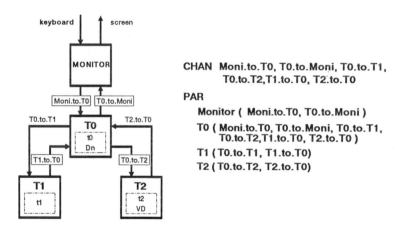

Fig 7.9 Occam Structure for VAP Control Law by using the Heuristic design approach

The resulting discrete functions corresponding to the Heuristic design approach of the VAP control law were mapped onto different transputer arrays varying from one up to three transputers, running concurrently. The occam structure used for this approach and the allocation of the equations, as three processes which are executed in parallel, is shown in Fig.7.9. This approach, like that of Parallel Branches, required a Monitor process to interface the input and output channels to the rest of the network.

In this program, the T0 process inputs data from the Monitor process and then sends this data simultaneously to T1 and T2. The T0 process evaluates Dn0, a partial result for the Dn calculation. Concurrently, the T1 and T2 processes are executed, and components Dn1, Dn2 and VD sent to the T0 process, which calculates Dn. Finally Dn and VD are broadcast to the Monitor process. These processes are repeated over each sample interval.

VAP CONTROL LAW : HEURISTIC APPROACH

Execution time for 1 transputer :   1.184 ms

Transputer	Processor Activity	Average Activity
1	100%	100%

Execution time for 2 transputers: 0.811 ms

Transputer	Processor Activity	Average Activity
1	97%	83%
2	69%	

Execution time for 3 transputers: 0.652 ms

Transputer	Processor Activity	Average Activity
1	91%	69%
2	55%	
3	61%	

Execution time for 4 transputers: 0.652ms

Transputer	Processor Activity	Average Activity
1	91%	52%
2	52%	
3	32%	
4	32%	

Table 7.2 Performance of the Heuristic design approach

The Heuristic design structure performance has been determined using the same timing tool utilized in the Parallel Branches approach. The average (%) transputer activity and execution time data are shown in Table 7.2 and refer to programs run on the IMS B003 board.

These results show an important reduction in the execution time when varying the number of transputers from one to three processors running concurrently. At the same time, there is a deterioration in the processor average activity. The last set of results shows that no further improvement could be obtained by adding a fourth transputer due to the presence of critical sequential paths.

7.3.1.3 Comparison of results

The performance of both the Parallel Branches and Heuristic design approaches is compared in Fig.7.10. For the Parallel Branches method, there is a significant improvement in execution time with high processor activity as more transputers are added. However, there is a tradeoff between activity and execution time. It can be seen that the Parallel Branches design has a slower execution time, using up to four transputers, than that achieved by the corresponding Heuristic approach. This is due to duplicaton of computation effort arising from the occurrence of common factors through this mapping approach. On the other hand, it realizes a higher processor activity due to its flexibility and the execution speed can be further increased by the addition of more transputers.

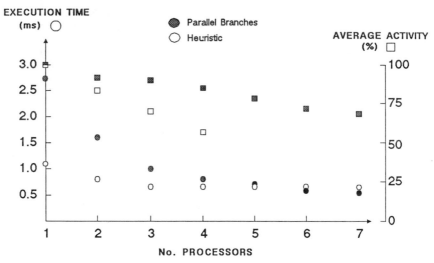

Fig 7.10 Parallel Branches and Heuristic approaches performance

The Heuristic approach has demonstrated the advantages related to simplicity and transparency in the mapping of the control law using up to three transputers to represent this structure. However, it is not possible to improve the performance using more transputers, due to the presence of critical sequential paths. Nevertheless, applying the Heuristic design to a 3-transputer array, this approach is faster than that achieved using the corresponding Parallel Branches approach with 3 transputers, even though the average activity of the Heuristic structure is worse than the Parallel Branches design.

These results suggest that an approach, based initially on the Heuristic method, followed by application of the Parallel Branches method to critical sections, might yield an effective solution.

7.3.1.4 Alternative configurations

The existing tree topology used to map the controller onto a transputer array suffers from the susceptibility of the master-slave structure to the potential failure of the master process. New designs, therefore, should seek to enable the processors to act as either master or slave in the event of failure. In this case, each transputer must be able to access the necessary software to service either role. Furthermore, each processor should be able to re-organise to assume a greater portion of the processing task in the resulting system. Another possible failure scenario might be the loss of a sensor or actuator service. Here, it would seem to be the role of the control law designer to produce alternative designs to accommodate such failures and accordingly exploit the processing power.

7.3.2 VAP Control Law Hardware

The next stage in the Demonstrator project was to realise hardware for the implementation of the control law on the BAC 1-11 test aircraft at RAE, Bedford. A VMEbus interface was designed so that an existing VMEbus microprocessor board on the aircraft could exchange data between a VMEbus analog input/output board and a transputer array. Fig.7.11 shows a block diagram of the interface interconnecting the data acquisition system and a transputer-based multiprocessor array.

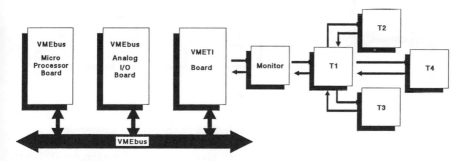

Fig 7.11 Block diagram of the VMEbus data acquisition system and the transputer array interfacing via the VMETI.

The microprocessor board is a Motorola MVME-101, double-height VMEbus card, which integrates a MC68000 16-bit microprocessor running at 8 MHz, 8 Kbytes of static RAM, 32 kBytes of EPROM, a timer, 2 RS232 ports and parallel i/o ports. This board has a Master configuration according to the VMEbus standard.

The analog input/output board is a Burr-Brown MPV-901A, double-height VMEbus card. The analog input includes 32 single-ended or 16 differential channels, a resistor programmed instrumentation amplifier, a sample/hold amplifier and 12-bit ADC. The analog output integrates two 12-bit DAC's and associated control logic. This board has a Slave configuration.

The microprocessor board acquires 6 data values from the 6 input channels of the MPV-901A board, scales them and stores them on off-board memory locations. Then it reads 2 data values from off-board memory locations and transfers them to MPV-901A output channels.

For the implementation of the VMEbus transputer interface, two designs were produced. The most successful design uses a dual-port RAM accessible to the transputer array and the VMEbus. An on-board dedicated 6502 microprocessor, transfers data from an IMS C011 link adaptor (configured in mode 2), connected to the transputer-based network, to the dual-port RAM, which functions as local memory for the 6502 system. This data can be accessed via the VMEbus by the M68000 processor system which handles the data exchange with the input/output board. The interface is double-height VMEbus card size. A block diagram of the interface is shown in Fig.7.12.

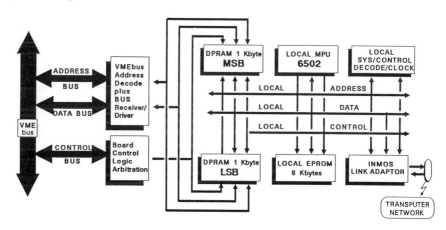

Fig 7.12 VMEbus Transputer Interface (VMETI) block diagram

The maximum speed of the interface exchanging data between the DPRAM and link adaptor is 1.8 ms. In a more advanced system, the 6502 microprocessor running at 1 MHz can be replaced by a 68000 processor running at 8MHz and the single link adaptor design of the interface can be upgraded by using two link adaptors for sending and receiving 12-bit data values in a single data transfer instruction. This would obviously increase the speed of updating data on the complete system.

The complete system has been proven to perform satisfactorily under laboratory conditions. A full flight test of the hardware is planned to be undertaken in 1988.

7.4 INVERSE DYNAMICS EQUATIONS FOR ROBOTIC CONTROL

The rigid body dynamics of a robot manipulator may be written [4]:

$$\mathbf{T} = M(\theta)\,\ddot{\theta} + V(\theta,\dot{\theta}) + G(\theta),$$

(7.9)

where

$M(\theta)$ is the mass matrix of the manipulator,
$V(\theta,\dot{\theta})$ is a vector of centrifugal and Coriolis terms,
$G(\theta)$ is a vector of gravity terms and
$\mathbf{T}$ is a vector of joint actuator torques.

From equation (7.9) it is evident that the moment of inertia seen by each joint actuator changes with its configuration. Furthermore, each succeeding link on the manipulator exerts varying gravitational, centrifugal and Coriolis forces on the preceding link. In a fast moving arm, the magnitudes of these terms are significant and unacceptable arm vibration can occur unless speeds are limited.

The control law can be partitioned by defining:

$$\mathbf{T} = M(\theta)\,\mathbf{T}^T + [V(\theta,\dot{\theta}) + G(\theta)],$$

(7.10)

Clearly, by substituting (7.10) into (7.9), the dynamic equations reduce to

$$\ddot{\theta} = \mathbf{T}^T$$

(7.11)

We form the errors:

$$\mathbf{e} = (\theta_d - \theta) \text{ and } \mathbf{e} = (\dot{\theta}_d - \dot{\theta})$$

(7.12)

where θ_d and $\dot{\theta}_d$ are demanded arm angles and rates, respectively, provided by a trajectory planner.

Then the control law can be written:

$$\mathbf{T}^T = \ddot{\theta}_d + K_v\,\mathbf{e} + K_p\,\mathbf{e} = \ddot{\theta},$$

(7.13)

where $\ddot{\theta}_d$ are the demanded joint accelerations.

The error equation is then:

$$\ddot{e} + K_v \dot{e} + K_p e = 0$$

(7.14)

from which appropriate values for K_v and K_p are easily chosen. This form of control system is shown in Fig.7.13.

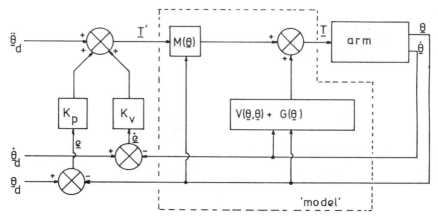

$\underline{\theta}$ is a vector of joint angles

Fig.7.13 Partitioned system for manipulator control

The model-based portion of the control system is a linearising and decoupling law which computes the torques actually applied at the manipulator's actuators to give the effect of the 'dummy' torques, $\mathbf{T}^T$. We note that there are difficulties associated with this type of embedded model control law:

(a) the parameters of the model may not be known accurately,

(b) the parameters may change (e.g. by the robot grasping an object) and

(c) terms may be missing from the model - joint friction and drive compliance, typically.

Decoupling and linearising will not be exact but, with reasonable parameter estimates, the gross effects of centrifugal and Coriolis forces will be compensated. Thus higher values of feedback gain can be used than with independent joint control giving improved performance over the operational range.

Much interest is now being shown in the parallel computation of this algorithm and here we investigate the potential of the transputer in this application.

7.4.1 Inverse Dynamics

The model-based part of the control law is known as the inverse dynamics. It is a calculation which must be carried out in real time, the sampling rate usually being set well above the bending mode frequencies of the manipulator. For example, Nigam and Lee [5] estimate that, in the case of a six-link PUMA robot, the sample time should be about 1.5ms.

The Newton-Euler (NE) formulation of inverse dynamics [4] is essentially a set of recursive formulae which are evaluated for each of the robot's links in turn, beginning at the base. Using the measured Euler variables, the angular and linear velocities and the total moments and forces exerted on each link are computed in a reverse recursion. Subsequently, the link-to-link reaction moments and the necessary joint torques (**T**) are calculated in a forward recursion. The full set of equations are lengthy and quoted elsewhere [7]. Here, we simply illustrate the problem of achieving parallelism within the algorithm by considering the first three such equations to be computed for each link:

angular velocity:

$$^{i}\underline{\omega}_i = A^{i-1}{}_i \, . \, ^{i-1}\underline{\omega}_{i-1} + z_i \, q_i$$

$$(7.15)$$

angular acceleration:

$$^{i}\underline{\dot{\omega}}_i = [\,^{i-1}\underline{\dot{\omega}}_{i-1} + z_i \, \dot{q}_i + \,^{i-1}\underline{\omega}_{i-1} \, . \, (z_i \, \dot{q}_i)]$$

$$(7.16)$$

linear velocity:

$$^{i}v_i = \,^{i}\underline{\omega}_i \, . \, ^{i}p_i + A^{i-1}{}_i \, . \, ^{i-1}v_{i-1}$$

$$(7.17)$$

Here we see that equations (7.15) and (7.16) for joint i must await information from the previous joint. Similarly, equation (7.17) must await information from the previous joint but also needs the result of eqn. (7.15).

7.4.2 One Processor per Link

In [6], Jones and Entwistle described a method of distributing the NE equations with a fixed allocation of one processor per robot link (typically six links). Each processor would receive computed values associated with the movement of the preceding link, compute the corresponding values for its own link, then pass these to the next processor to continue the recursion. This fixed correspondence between a joint and its processor leads to loss of parallelism. For example, although equations (7.15) and (7.16) above could be computed concurrently they cannot in this case since they are allocated to the same processor. A simulation of this scheme [6] showed that the processor utilisation was indeed poor in terms of speedup and concurrency.

7.4.3 Processor Farm

The concept of a processor farm involves a set of 'worker' processors being allocated the tasks to be executed (on-line), the data flow being coordinated by a 'master' processor. The architecture is outlined in Fig.7.14.

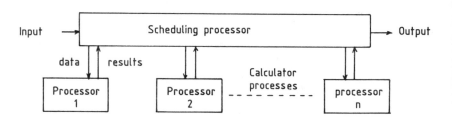

Fig.7.14 Structure for on-line scheduling

In this case, each equation of the NE algorithm is considered to be a task which may be allocated to ANY one of the processors once all the data required for evaluation is available. This architecture possesses some desirable properties:

(a) It is relatively easy to increase the number of processors used

(b) Failure tolerance is easier to implement, i.e. the demise of one processor degrades the system rather than causing total failure

(c) It improves speedup and concurrency.

7.4.4 Simulation

The performance of this scheme was investigated by **simulation** before undertaking a full software development. For each of the tasks a typical execution time was estimated by counting floating point operations. The precedence relationships for the execution of a given task are specified as a list of other tasks which will supply its data.

Once the task set has been defined, the simulation package allows the user to vary the number of processors available and to select various forms of scheduling criteria. The simulation produces execution times for the total task set and the average processor activity.

Various scheduling criteria have been investigated, such as first-come, first-served (FIFO), and a priority based selection scheme (MDDPS - maximum depth dependent priority scheduling). The latter is constructed by counting, for any given task, the number of 'task levels' which depend on its result. Those tasks with high dependence counts receive priority allocation in the case of contention for available processors. This data is easily generated off-line.

7.4.5 Results of Simulation

We chose to analyse the well-known Stanford arm [7] which requires 543 flops per pass. We also assumed a 50ns T414-20 transputer which has quoted $+/*$ times of 11.5/11.0 μs respectively for floating point operations performed by a set of occam routines.

Fig.7.15(a) shows the execution time versus the number of processors (n). The ideal curve, giving an absolute lower bound, is the 1/n speed-up. The FIFO scheduler gives good performance and reaches a critical time at around 14 processors. The critical time for any given task set is reached when there are sufficient processors available to exhaust the parallelism within the set.

Using MDDPS achieves a substantial improvement in execution time and processor efficiency. Fig.7.15(b) shows that, up to the critical time, the average processor activity is better than 93%. The critical number of processors is 8 after which no further improvement can be obtained by adding more processors.

We remark here that a single 68020/68881 combination (approx. 3.0 μs per flop) would take 1.6ms to complete this computation (equivalent to 4 T414's) while a single T800-20 (approx. 0.5 μs per flop) would take 0.27ms!

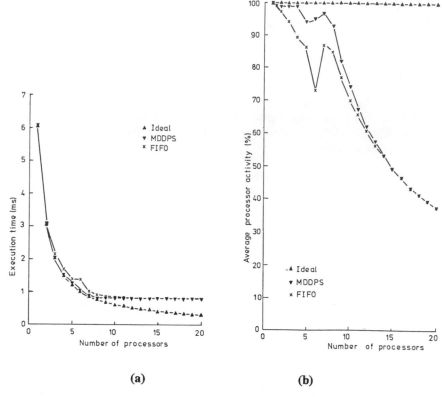

(a)   (b)

**Fig.7.15   (a) Variation of execution time with number of processors
(b) Variation of average processor activity with number of processors**

7.4.6 Estimating Overheads

The simulation results are encouraging, but are limited by the omission of the overheads for generating the real-time schedule and the inter-processor communications. At present we are investigating the impact of these overheads by means of timing measurements on a multi-transputer system (B004/B003 boards). The structure chosen is a processor 'farm' as shown in Fig.7.16.

The initial measurements showed that the scheduling process itself took longer than the computation of tasks! Re-coding this process yielded substantial improvement but the time taken was still comparable to the task computation time, thus destroying any speed-up due to parallelism.

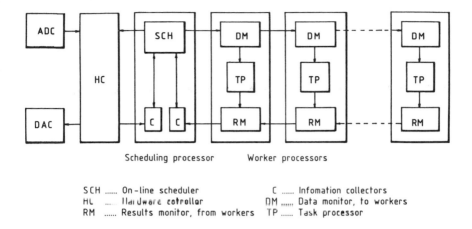

Scheduling processor   Worker processors

SCH ...... On-line scheduler   C ...... Infomation collectors
HC ...... Hardware cotrollor   DM ,,,,,, Data monitor, to workers
RM ...... Results monitor, from workers   TP ...... Task processor

Fig.7.16 An example architecture of a processor farm with scheduling

Communications overheads were investigated by using pre-determined schedules to eliminate the scheduler overhead. The difference between the measured and simulated times was attributable to communications between the processors. Again this turned out to be substantial, since detailed measurements showed that the **effective** data rate across INMOS links (especially with the small 'packets' used in this application) are much slower than the quoted 20 Mbit/s. Again, the performance of the farm was found to be sensitive to the method of occam coding used.

7.4.7 Conclusions

We conclude that the inverse dynamics equations are amenable to parallel processing despite their recursive nature. Simple scheduling techniques, on low numbers of processors can potentially yield good speed-up and efficiency.

This conclusion is tempered by our experience with the timing performance achieved on multiple transputers, with all the processes written in software. The difficulty is caused by the scale of timing that we wish to achieve, in this case being constrained by a fairly fast sampling time of around 1ms. Such a constraint will, of course, be typical of real-time control systems. We surmise that, given a problem with ten times as much computation - and ten times as much time to accomplish it - the overheads would not be as serious. Indeed this is why the transputer, used in very large arrays, is so impressive in its performance on hideously compute-bound problems such as Mandelbrot generation and ray-tracing.

Presently, then, we are faced with the tantalising results of a simulation that shows the potential power of parallel processing but realise that the real challenge is to release the arithmetic power of the transputer on short timescales. To this end we now intend to investigate:

- other forms of processor farm architecture
- development of a hardware scheduler
- faster communications by means of the memory interface.

ACKNOWLEDGEMENTS

This work was partly performed under SERC grant GR/D/65749. R.A.E., Bedford supported the flight controller work.

The authors would like to thank the members of the Bangor Control Software Group for their contributions to this work. Collaborators at R.A.E., Bedford (E. Bailey and G. Ingle), BAe (Brough) and GEC Research (Leicester) have made many useful suggestions as the projects progressed.

REFERENCES

1. Matsuo, T. and Lipo, T.A., 1985, "A rotor parameter identification scheme for vector controlled induction motor drives", IEEE Trans. Ind. App., Vol.IA-21, (4), pp.624-632.

2. Harasima, F., et al., 1985, "Multimicroprocessor based control system for quick response induction motor drive", IEEE Trans. Ind. App., Vol.IA-21, (4), pp.602-609.

3. Goddard, K.F. and Cooke, N., 1980, "Flight trials of an automatic control law for a BAC 1-11 Aircraft", Technical Report 80003, Royal Aircraft Establishment.

4. Craig, J.J., 1986, "Introduction to Robotics: Mechanics & Control", Addison-Wesley.

5. Nigam R. and Lee, C.S.G., 1985, "A multiprocessor based controller for the control of mechanical manipulators", Trans. IEEE RA-1 (4), pp.173-182.

6. Jones, D.I. and Entwistle, P.M., 1986, "A parallel processor approach to the inverse dynamics problem of a robot manipulator", Proc. 10th Annual Microcomputer Applications Workshop, University of Strathclyde.

7. Paul, R.P., 1981, "Robot manipulators: Mathematics, programming and control", MIT Press, Cambridge Mass.

Chapter 8

Software fault tolerance in real-time systems

Dr. D.J. Holding & Dr. G.F. Carpenter

8.1 INTRODUCTION

The software for a modern real-time programmable system will typically comprise a set of interacting processes which are distributed over a suitable processing architecture.

The starting point for the design of such a system is the derivation of the system requirements specification. The specification should state what the system should do in a formal and precise manner. However, the requirements specification should not state how the task should be carried out nor how it should be implemented.

The requirements specification is normally translated into a design by a process of elaboration in which the description of what the system should do is elaborated until the description comprises a set of easily implemented activities. In most design methods, the formal system specification will be analysed and decomposed on a functional basis. Careful consideration should be given to determining when to take decisions which bind or constrain the design, such as the choice of programming notation or processing architecture. The design procedure often consists of a compromise between taking an early decision to map the problem onto a known implementation, such as a particular high-performance architecture, or delaying such decisions to retain the freedom of choice in design and implementation.

It is desirable that the process of analysis is not subject to implementation constraints before the analysis has revealed the characteristics of the problem. For example, the analysis should reveal those parts of the system which comprise concurrent activities, and those which are strictly sequential, before the decision is taken on how these activities should be implemented. This is particularly important if the designer is to exploit fully the advantages which can be obtained by using modern concurrent programming notations and processing hardware, such as Occam [1] and the Transputer [2].

In applications which involve safety functions or have implications for safety, the system must perform in a reliable and safe manner. Ideally, the designer should prove the correctness of the design and the design should be translated into an implementation using proven translators. Finally, the implementation should be verified to show that it is fit for its intended use. However, current formal proof techniques require high levels of skill; they are also lengthy and are not efficient for complex systems.

To overcome this difficulty, a designer may consider using software fault tolerance in the design of a system. The aim is to design a system which will meet its specification in the presence of certain classes of fault. The fault tolerance can be built into the system during the design process to protect a specific process or set of processes. Software fault tolerance techniques are normally applied economically, perhaps to protect a specific function of the system.

The design of fault tolerant sequential software is relatively straightforward and well developed. The design of fault tolerant concurrent software is much more complex because an error can migrate between processes through inter-process actions which can not be revoked. The fault tolerant design must bound the scope of such a fault and must provide an error recovery mechanism in which the processes affected by the fault co-operate to recover from an error.

This Chapter describes the characteristics and performance of real-time sequential and concurrent software, because this is fundamental to the behaviour of the software under normal and fault conditions. The Chapter also describes the main fault tolerant techniques and explains how they can be applied to sequential, concurrent and real-time systems. It outlines methods for the design of such systems, and explains how these designs can be implemented and verified. Reference is made to the application of these techniques and to areas of current research.

8.2 NATURE OF SEQUENTIAL AND CONCURRENT PROCESSES

8.2.1 Characteristics

8.2.1.1 Sequential processes

Imperative programming languages provide notations for the expression of algorithms. Programs written in such languages prescribe what has to be done and the sequence in which the task is to be carried out.

In the design process for a sequential system, the problem is analysed and a sequential order is imposed on the problem to yield a sequential design that is compatible with the proposed implementation. The solution will comprise six primitive constructs which are to be found in all sequential programming languages [3]:
- sequence
- input

- output
- assignment
- selection (decision)
- repetition (iteration)

We have seen that these constructs correspond to the six sequential constructs in Occam, (**SEQ, ?, !, :=, IF, WHILE**), with the proviso that input and output comprise synchronous communications to other (external) processes.

8.2.1.2 Real-time processes

Many engineering systems, such as embedded computer real-time systems, are required to maintain synchronism with an asynchronous external system, or to respond to stimuli from such a system, within a finite and specifiable delay. In real-time programming there is a primary need for a mechanism for handling the concept of time. Real-time sequential programming languages include an additional primitive construct which allows the formal inclusion of time.

Occam provides a local sense of time by means of a real-time time-counter. A process may read the current value of the counter (**TIME ?** value) or wait until the counter exceeds a given value (**TIME ? AFTER** value).

8.2.1.3 Concurrent processes

In the design process, concurrency can be included at both the software and hardware level. Therefore, important design decisions have to be taken on the extent to which concurrency should be used in the design of:

- the software processes,
- the processing architecture (over which the software processes will be distributed).

This Chapter is concerned primarily with the design of software processes.

Concurrent imperative programming languages, such as Modula-2, Concurrent Pascal, Ada and Occam, provide notations for the expression of concurrency. Programs written in such languages prescribe what has to be done, describe the set of sequential and concurrent processes which will carry out the task, and describe the actions and interactions of these processes. This is possible only if a problem can be analysed to give a concurrent design.

Programming notations for the description of loosely-coupled real-time concurrent systems normally comprise the seven primitive constructs which are to be found in all real-time sequential programming languages, and two additional primitive constructs for describing concurrency [3].

8.2.1.4 Parallel processes and synchronisation

The simplest concurrent construct is that which initiates a number of processes in parallel, such as the Occam PAR construct. Each parallel process runs asynchronously and then terminates. The construct does not terminate until all the parallel processes have terminated.

8.2.1.5 Inter-process communications

All concurrent programming languages provide facilities for defining inter-process actions. These typically include communications via shared variables and/or communications by message passing.

The communicating processes are mutually asynchronous if the read and write operations on shared variables are asynchronous, if the interprocess action comprises separate one-way communications such as send and receive messages, or if a single inter-process message may be left in a message buffer such that the sender does not need to wait for the receiving process. Asynchronous communications are not supported in Occam at the primitive level.

The communicating processes are forced into mutual synchronisation if the action of communication is an atomic, two-way action. This will be so if a communication between the processes, across a named unidirectional channel, can only take place when the predefined input and output processes are both ready. For example, synchronisation by message passing is supported in Occam by the pair of synchronous input and output primitives (? !).

Synchronisation by message passing enforces a strict discipline on the designer because errors in the synchronisation logic will lead to deadlock. The more flexible constraints associated with asynchronous communications would appear to offer a design advantage. However, the additional effort needed to design a synchronous system is often more than compensated by the reduction in the effort needed to test the system because such systems are more amenable to analysis, as shown in Section 8.2.2.

8.2.1.6 Asynchronous processes and races

Non-deterministic selective communications, such as those which occur when a number of processes compete for access to a non-pre-emptive resource, are normally accommodated by use of guarded processes [4]. For example, Occam makes use of synchronous communications between processes to support guarded alternative processes (the **ALT** construct). This construct offers a set of alternative processes for execution, each guarded by a synchronous input (or a synchronous input in conjunction with a Boolean expression, or the special SKIP primitive which is always ready). The first guard to be satisfied enables its protected process for execution; the other processes are not enabled and will not be executed.

Particular care must be exercised when an ALT construct is used to form an asynchronous race between processes, as in the case of two processes competing for access to a resource. The race is won by the first process to satisfy the guard. However, once the race is completed, the losing process will deadlock unless the design ensures that the outstanding communication (requesting the resource) from the losing process is satisfied elsewhere.

8.2.1.7 Deadlock

In Chapter 5.9 we saw that deadlock occurs when an active process is waiting for an event which will not occur. In communicating sequential processes, such as those described in Occam, a process is deadlocked when it is waiting for a synchronous communication from another process which is unable to be party to the communication.

Deadlock typically arises from poor design. For example, the losing process in an asynchronous race will be deadlocked unless its communication for the resource is satisfied. Deadlock will also arise if a crude attempt is made to abort a process, such as might be required following a timeout in a real-time system. Similar problems may arise from the careless use of the selective constructs. For example, consider a selection process which chooses between two processes, one of which contains a communication, such that the communication will take place only if the selection condition is true. If the condition is false, then the communication will not take place and the process which expects the communication will be deadlocked unless it too checks the same condition. Deadlock can often be detected at an early stage by using software modelling, simulation and animation tools. It can also be prevented by careful design.

Deadlock may also occur after a failure, such as the failure of a process to generate a required output, or the occurrence of a fault which leads to the failure of a process or a communication link. These matters are considered further in Sections 8.3 and 8.4.

8.2.1.8 Distributed decision mechanisms

Synchronous communication primitives provide a useful method of enforcing synchronism between processes through communications. These primitives can also be used to construct communication protocols for the various types of inter-process transactions required in control applications, such as generating commands, eliciting status, or annunciating alarms [5].

Many concurrent control applications involve making distributed (multi-party) decisions. If two or more processes are involved in a transaction, or a set of concurrent transactions, then it may be necessary to use concurrency control techniques to ensure that each transaction is atomic and the results of a set of concurrent transactions are consistent (i.e. the same as if the transactions were executed sequentially). For example, two-phase commit protocols, or non-blocking three-phase commit protocols can be used to ensure that either all processes perform their part of a transaction or no process performs any part of the transaction [6,7]. These protocols can be constructed using synchronous communication primitives and appropriate non-deadlocking transaction-abortion mechanisms [8].

8.2.2 Analysis and Synthesis Tools

As we have seen, Occam provides the minimum set of constructs necessary for the design of loosely coupled, distributed, real-time systems. It allows the designer to incorporate concurrency naturally into the design. Occam also provides logic structures, such as synchronous inter-process communications, which allow the designer to generate deterministic systems in which process execution is co-ordinated through inter-process communications. Equally important, the mathematical foundation of CSP, on which Occam is based, provides an underlying mathematical structure which can be used in the formal specification of the system and in the synthesis and verification of the design, including any fault tolerant structures.

8.2.2.1 State models

Concurrent programs written in deterministic languages, such as Occam, can be modelled as networks of states and state transitions. The system variables are modelled by the network states and the state transitions correspond to the changes of state as each primitive process, or complex of processes, is executed. Therefore, the dynamics of the system will be characterised by the evolution of the system states through a sequence of state transitions.

Considerable work has been done on the modelling of state transition networks using, for example, Petri nets. Petri nets can be used to model asynchronous and synchronous logic systems [9]. They can also be used to model sequential and concurrent software [10]. The resulting state space representation can be used to simulate process execution. This allows the designer to resolve many state reachability problems and to obtain important information about the dynamic behaviour and performance of the constituent processes.

8.2.2.1.1 Sequential processes

A sequential process can be represented by a Petri net by associating each process state with a Petri net place, and each state transition with a Petri net transition. For a single, strictly sequential process, each transition has a single entry place and a single exit place and process execution can be simulated by a single marking token flowing through the Petri net. A transition is enabled if its input place is marked and execution of the Petri net proceeds by firing those transitions which are enabled. Petri net representations can be generated for all the sequential constructs in Occam.

The graphical representation of a Petri net model provides a useful medium in which to illustrate concepts and analytical results. However, in more complex cases, the Petri net is usually analysed using set theory. This analysis is, of course, normally automated.

8.2.2.1.2 Concurrent processes

Petri nets can be used also to model deterministic concurrent processes, and Petri net representation can be generated for all the concurrent constructs in Occam, including synchronous inter-process communications [11]. These concurrent models are naturally more complex than the models of sequential software. The generation of each parallel process results in the creation of an additional marking token which flows through that process until the process terminates whereupon the token is eliminated. Thus, concurrent execution is represented by the flow of more than one token in the Petri net.

Models of concurrent software can be used in simulations of the execution of the software and in investigations of whether the system is free from deadlock. The net may also be represented by the underlying set theory, provided it complies with certain (non-onerous) constraints. In complex cases, it is often simpler to use set theory to investigate the net.

8.2.2.1.3 Real-time processes

Petri net models can be generated for the real-time constructs in Occam. In these models, the local sense of time is represented by an external input which forces time-synchronism on the receiving process through a synchronous (input) communication.

8.2.2.2 Inter-process actions

The state transitions can be classified as either inter-process actions or intra-process actions.

Inter-process actions involve synchronous communications between processes and provide the mechanism for synchronising a concurrent system. Thus, inter-process actions are critical to the behaviour of the whole system. Formal methods or simulation studies are commonly used to ensure that the inter-process actions are specified properly and implemented correctly. Unfortunately, inter-process actions also provide a mechanism for fault migration. Therefore, inter-process actions should only be used sparsely as part of carefully controlled inter-process dialogues.

Intra-process actions are local to a process and do not directly affect other processes. When analysing a design using Petri nets, considerable simplification can be obtained by reducing sets of intra-process actions to a single (complex) intra-process action.

Further reductions in complexity can be obtained by using techniques for handling complexity, such as partitioning. For example, a system can be partitioned into a hierarchical set of processes, and the system communications can be classified as intra-process or inter-process communications with respect to the chosen set of boundaries. This technique is most useful when the partition or boundary is designed to exploit the structural characteristics of the system. For example, this type of classification can be used in the design of fault tolerant mechanisms to protect a particular process, as discussed in Section 8.3.3.5.

8.2.2.3 Attributes of processes

The functional boundaries of a distributed system can be mapped onto an Occam model of the system. They can also be mapped onto the Petri net. Thus each process in the model can be associated with a particular function and can be given a function-identifier attribute. These attributes can be used to identify all those processes which are party to a particular function or all those functions which are influenced directly by a particular process. It is then possible to discriminate between intra-function and inter-function communications. These function-boundaries can be used in the design of fault tolerant mechanisms which protect a particular function, as shown in Section 8.3.3.5.

8.2.2.4 State reachability, state activity and deadlock

Deterministic concurrent systems, including fault tolerant systems, can be modelled using Petri nets. The dynamic behaviour of such systems is defined by the sequence of state transitions which take place from a given initial state (or marking) of the Petri net. Thus, the behaviour of the system can be analysed by tracing tokens as they flow through the net. This analysis is normally carried out using reachability sets.

The reachability set is those markings which are potentially reachable from a given initial marking. The reachability set can be represented conventionally as a tree, where the nodes of the tree are markings and the arcs of the tree are transitions which must fire to arrive at the given marking. In simple cases, the reachability tree can be analysed by inspection. In general, the number of reachable markings can be very large and the analysis of the reachability set is usually performed by computer. Analysis of the reachability set allows the designer to determine which transition sequences are live, whether any given marking is reachable, and whether the net is prone to deadlock.

8.2.2.5 Complexity

The use of the Petri net in the analysis of concurrent software gives useful performance gains because each software process is reduced to a single transition. To keep the analysis manageable it is often necessary to attempt to bound the net by using specific programming techniques and to reduce the complexity of the net by applying net-reduction techniques. However, the analysis is still subject to the problem of combinatorial explosion.

8.3 SOFTWARE FAULT TOLERANCE

8.3.1 Principles of Fault Tolerance

The design of concurrent real-time software which is reliable and safe is a most demanding task. The designer normally tries to avoid introducing errors into the design by adopting an appropriate design methodology based on sound mathematical principles [12]. Thus, a specification will be developed using a formal notation. This representation will be strict, so that no misinterpretation can occur. The specification will then be translated into a design using property-preserving (error-free) transformations. Ideally, the methodology will include procedures and tools for:

- the formal specification of the system,
- the automatic translation of the formal specifications into a design,
- the implementation of the design,
- the verification of the system,
- the documentation of the design,
- the maintenance of the software.

In general, those methodologies which do exist are either not yet widely adopted or have limited scope and require manual procedures [13]. Thus, despite modern techniques, specification and design errors may still be introduced into designs, and may contribute to the growing catalogue of faults and failures which have occurred in complex systems [14].

8.3.1.1 Errors and faults

Errors in the specification or design of a system will lead to software faults ("bugs") which will lie hidden within the system until a particular instantiation of the system state activates the fault and generates a error; the error may lead to the failure of the system.

The number of faults in a piece of software does not increase with age, nor does the nature of a software fault change with age if the operational environment is invariant. Thus, the process of ageing of software is different from the process of ageing of hardware. This is shown by the statistic for the occurrence of errors [15]:

the rate of occurrence of errors is highest during the development or early life of the software and, if the faults are corrected, the rate of occurrence of software errors decreases throughout the life of the product.

8.3.1.2 Redundancy and fault tolerance

Fault tolerance can be used to limit the scope of faults or to mask errors so that they do not lead to failure. Fault tolerance involves the use of redundancy to give the system resilience [16,17,18,19].

8.3.1.2.1 Fault masking

The most common fault-tolerant technique, N-modular redundancy [16], involves the n-fold replication of processes or systems. The replicated processes are operated in parallel and the results computed by the variant paths are compared. If an error is generated by any one path, it will be detected and the erroneous result will be suppressed, thus masking the fault.

N-modular redundancy is characterised by the massive redundancy of software (and often of hardware). In the software version of this technique, N-version programming, the usual replication factor is 3 and diverse techniques are used in the programming of the triplicated paths.

8.3.1.2.2 Error detection and recovery mechanisms

Error detection and recovery techniques provide an alternative approach to software fault tolerance. The aim of the method is to detect an error, to assess the damage caused by the error, and to initiate an error recovery mechanism in order to compute an error-free result with the minimum delay. The method is characterised by the economical use of redundant software.

Two recovery techniques are commonly used. The forward error recovery method [20, 21] aims to minimise delay by transforming the erroneous state directly into a correct or acceptable state. In many cases a previously computed acceptable value, or a default value, is used to replace an erroneous value in the erroneous state. In the alternative method, backward error recovery, the system backtracks through previous states until it can restore a previously computed correct state and restart processing in the forward direction. Following the restart, a diverse forward path is often used to save time or to avoid a common mode error in the forward path.

8.3.2 Software Fault Tolerance in Sequential Systems

A number of fault tolerant mechanisms have been proposed for both sequential and concurrent systems. The problem of designing fault tolerant software for real-time systems is much simpler for sequential systems than for concurrent systems, because error migration in the sequential system is bound by the lack of inter-process communication channels. This makes it easier to design appropriate error detection and recovery mechanisms such as recovery blocks [22,23].

8.3.2.1   Recovery block scheme and the ensure notation

The recovery block is a fundamental structure for fault tolerance in sequential systems. A design notation for the recovery block scheme is given below [23]:

```
ensure   acceptance test AT
   by   process P
   else by   process Q
   else by   default;
```

Before entry to the block, a copy of the system state is saved. This state is assumed to be error free. The process P within the recovery block is then executed. The results from process P are assessed using the acceptance-test AT. If the results are acceptable, the system is assumed to be error free and execution passes out of the recovery block. If the results from P are unacceptable, then the system backtracks, restores the entry state, and recomputes the task using the diverse process Q. Normally the results from Q will be acceptable. However, it is necessary to include a default process which always generates acceptable results to ensure that the block terminates.

8.3.2.2   Implementation of a recovery block

A recovery block can be implemented using the following, easily extensible, design:

```
procedure recovery(i : integer);
   ...
   function AT : boolean;
   ...
   begin
      ....
      establish recovery point;
      i := 0;
      repeat
        i := i + 1;
        case i of
          1 : P ;
          2 : begin  recovery (i); Q ;   end;
          3 : begin  recovery (i); default;   end
        end;
      until AT;
      ...
   end.
```

8.3.2.3 Control applications

N-version programming and recovery block techniques have been used successfully to provide software fault tolerance for sequential systems [23,24]. Recovery blocks have also been used in conjunction with watchdog timers to provide fault tolerance in real-time systems. This technique has been used to guard against certain classes of transient hardware faults [25].

8.3.3 Software Fault Tolerance in Concurrent Systems

8.3.3.1 Nature of faults in concurrent systems

The recovery block technique for error detection and recovery in sequential systems requires considerable modification if it is to be applied to networks of communicating sequential processes because errors can propagate between processes through interprocess interactions which cannot be revoked. Error detection mechanisms for distributed systems must take into account the promulgation of errors in their assessment of error damage. Also, the error recovery scheme must involve all processes which may have been affected by the error. It follows that the structure of the inter-process actions in a distributed system is central to the design of the fault tolerant mechanism.

8.3.3.2 Dynamic and static recovery methods, the domino effect

Software fault tolerance for a distributed system may be provided by suitably extending the recovery block technique. The method involves partitioning the set of concurrent processes into groups of processes which will co-operate in error detection and recovery. However, the partitioning must not be performed arbitrarily because the backtracking recovery operation must be a properly co-ordinated procedure involving all the concurrent processes which are party to an error. Unless the recovery is carefully controlled, and its scope is bound, the action of recovery may extend beyond the proposed recovery block and may lead to progressive collapse of the whole system (the domino effect) [23].

If the recovery operation is to be limited in extent, then it is necessary to identify partitions or a boundary within the state-space of the distributed system which can be used for error detection and recovery. The boundary must define the entry to, and exit from, a set of co-ordinated recovery blocks which limit the extent of the propagation of errors which arise within the boundary and the extent of backtracking under fault condition.

The conversation mechanism proposed by Randell [23] uses a particular form of closed boundary to define a recovery block for a general set of distributed processes. Identifying the boundary of a conversation for a set of communicating concurrent processes is not a trivial task because the state of each asynchronous process is independent of the state of other processes, except when the processes are forced into synchronism by interprocess communications. In general, it is not possible to determine a priori the particular sequence of states which will be instantiated when the software is executed. Therefore, the boundary must be identified dynamically or must be independent of the sequence of occurrence of the independent states.

The problem of the dynamic identification of conversation boundaries has been the subject of much research [26,27]. Considerable care is necessary in the design of such systems because dynamic recovery techniques may exhibit the domino effect. It will be necessary to show that specific dynamic recovery methods are free from the domino effect before these methods can be put to practical use.

8.3.3.3 Conversations

The conversation uses a co-ordinated set of recovery blocks to implement a distributed error detection and recovery mechanism. The boundary of the conversation consists of a recovery line, a test line and two side walls, which enclose the set of interacting processes which are party to the conversation.

The recovery line defines the start of the conversation. It consists of a co-ordinated set of states (recovery points), one for each participating process. On entry to the conversation, each process saves its entry state for later use should recovery be required. The participating processes need not enter the conversation simultaneously.

The sidewalls isolate the body of the conversation from other processes and no communications are allowed through these walls; this prevents any errors generated within the conversation being propagated to other processes.

The test line is a co-ordinated set of acceptance tests for the set of interacting processes. The co-ordinated acceptance test is normally a two stage procedure comprising local and global tests. Each test-line process must pass an acceptance test. If all processes pass their respective acceptance tests, a global acceptance test is carried out. If the global test is successful, the conversation is terminated and all processes exit synchronously. However, if any acceptance test (local or global) is failed, recovery must take place.

Recovery is achieved by rolling back the whole conversation to the recovery line, restoring the state of each process to that on entry, and executing a pre-defined alternative process or the default process. If the results from the alternative process are acceptable the conversation will terminate, otherwise the results from the default process will be used to exit the conversation. Thus all processes in the conversation co-operate in error detection and all participate in any subsequent recovery.

8.3.3.4 Static methods for the design of conversations

8.3.3.4.1 Dialogues

In general, software fault tolerance will be used to protect a particular process or function. If the protection is to be built-in automatically during the synthesis of the design, then the conversation and recovery mechanism must be included in the design specification. The conversation boundary will govern the design of the constituent processes and the inter-process actions (or dialogue between the processes). For example, particular care will have to be exercised to ensure that a proper set of recovery states are saved on entry to the conversation, that the inter-process actions do not violate the proposed sidewalls, and that exit from the conversation is controlled by a properly co-ordinated and synchronised test-line process.

The test-line process and recovery mechanism can be implemented as a centralised process. Alternatively, the decision process may be distributed among the constituent processes and implemented using multi-phase commit protocols (or structured dialogues) [28,29].

8.3.3.4.2 Conversation placement

Conversation placement is an alternative approach to the design of fault tolerant systems. In this method, the system is designed to the functional requirement. The design is then analysed in order to identify conversation boundaries which will protect particular processes or functions. The aim is to delay the point at which the conversation boundary is identified in order to give maximum flexibility in the design of the system. The objective is to select (or place) a boundary comprising a recovery line, side walls, and a test-line in such a way that the side walls coincide with natural partitions in the structure of the processes. The identification of such a boundary allows the conversation and its associated recovery mechanism to be implemented without disturbing the nature of the processes or their inter-process actions. This technique is described in Section 8.3.3.5.

8.3.3.5 Conversation design and placement

A method has been developed [30] which allows the systematic placement of conversations which protect specific processes or functions. The technique is based on the analysis of the inter-process actions associated with a specified process or function, because these provide the mechanism for the migration of errors.

The analysis of inter-process actions involves the use of Petri net models and state reachability techniques to identify those state changes which are caused by inter-process communications. The underlying structure of the communications can be captured using state-change tables. Inter-process and inter-function actions can be identified by examining the process-attributes or functional-attributes of the elements of the state change table. Also, the extent of allowable error migrations for the protection of a specific process or function can be determined by tracing the inter-process or inter-function communications following the error.

The aim is to identify proper conversation boundaries which bound the extent of error migration. Allowable migrations are enclosed within the boundary of the conversation while unwanted migrations are prevented by placing such communications beyond the test-line process. Such boundaries, and their associated entry and exit states, can be found by forming closed contours, which enclose all required processes, along any branch or sub-tree of the state change table. The recovery and exit states defined by such a boundary can be used directly in the design of the conversation, as described in Section 8.3.4.

The technique, which is known as boundary placement, can be used to determine boundaries which protect a specific process or protect all the processes associated with a particular function. The method can be automated (using the underlying set theory) and provides a systematic method for the placement of conversations, or properly nested sets of conversations. The method can also be used in the verification of conversations which have been developed by direct synthesis or dialogues.

8.3.4 The Design and Implementation of Conversations

The ensure notation described in Section 8.3.2 can be extended to distributed systems to provide a structure for the implementation of the conversation scheme.

The approach can be illustrated by considering the design of a fault tolerant mechanism for a distributed system [31] in which three concurrent processes p1, p2, and p3 form the components of a proper conversation P. The design problem is to embed the conversation comprising p1, p2, p3 within a fault tolerance framework which comprises a co-ordinated set of recovery points, a co-ordinated set of acceptance tests; and alternative processes 'Q' and 'default'.

The general structure of the solution will follow the solution given for the sequential recovery block in Section 8.3.2. However, in concurrent systems, the structure of the fault tolerant system can be simplified by computing the primary and alternative processes in parallel, as shown in the following occam description:

```
SEQ
   establish recovery point
   PAR
      PAR      -- conversation P
         p1
         p2
         p3
      Q
      default
   :
```

8.3.4.1 Recovery line processes

The recovery line processes are used to save the system state on entry to the conversation; this state is assumed to be error free. The general structure for each asynchronous recovery line processes follows that shown in Section 8.3.2.2 for sequential recovery blocks.

However, in the concurrent implementation described in Section 8.3.4.4, the primary process P and the alternative processes (Q and 'default') can be initiated in parallel with identical copies of the initial high integrity system states and all alternative processing can be computed in parallel. Therefore, there will be no need to establish a recovery point or a process roll-back mechanism.

8.3.4.2 Test line processes

The structure of the acceptance test requires careful design. In general, the acceptance test can be performed in two phases. In the first phase, local tests are carried out as each constituent process in the conversation (e.g. p1) produces partial results. If any local test indicates a fault, then the whole set of processes in the conversation (e.g. P) must be decreed faulty. However, local tests are not sufficient for an acceptance test of the whole conversation, and the local tests must be followed by a second phase of tests which assess the complete set of results. This requirement can be achieved by a centralised global acceptance test which assesses the complete set of results from the conversation (e.g. P).

The implementation is simplified if each constituent process of a conversation is associated with two additional processes: one to buffer the partial results and the second to perform the first (local) phase of acceptance testing. Thus, process p1 (which is a constituent of conversation P) passes its results to a local results-buffer, p1_buffer. On completion, p1 would initiate its local acceptance test, atp1, and then terminate (since it will play no further part in the conversation).

A similar structure is adopted in the second (global) phase of acceptance testing. The partial results from the component processes, once they have passed local acceptance tests, are passed to (and are managed by) a conversation-buffer process, p_conversation_buffer. When all the local acceptance tests for that conversation have been passed, the global acceptance test, atp_global, can be used to test the results assembled in the conversation buffer.

8.3.4.3   Distributed acceptance tests and backtracking

The global acceptance test is performed by the process atp_global and its decision is communicated to a centralised 'arbitrator' process : if the test is successful the conversation terminates.

However, if the results of primary process, P, fail the acceptance tests at either local or global levels, the results are discarded in their entirety and the results of the alternative processes are tested and used in the order specified by the 'ensure' notation. Since the results of P and of all alternative processing are computed in parallel, the results of the alternative process Q (if acceptable) or the 'default' process can be simply substituted. Therefore, there is no need to establish a recovery point or a process roll-back mechanism in the sequential sense.

The sequence in which results of the acceptance tests on the primary and alternate processes (conversations) are accepted is specified by the 'ensure' notation and is implemented by the centralised 'arbitrator' process. This process arbitrates between the acceptance tests from each conversation, selects which set of results to use and terminates the conversation.

The overall structure (at the outermost level) of the conversation implementation is illustrated below; superfluous PARs and SEQs are retained for clarity.

```
PAR
   PAR                 -- primary conversation
      PAR
         p1
         p1_buffer
         atp1
      PAR
         p2
         p2_buffer
         atp2
      PAR
         p3
         p3_buffer
         atp3
      p_conversation_buffer
      atp_global
   PAR                          -- alternative conversation
      q
      q_conversation_buffer
      atq
   PAR                      -- default conversation
      default
      default_buffer
   SEQ
      arbitrator
```

The channel linkage between these processes is illustrated in Fig.8.1. Heavily shaded lines indicate the flow of data. The local acceptance tests, atp1,2,3, control the flow of data (no/no-go) from the local results buffers associated with the component processes to the conversation results buffer and then onward to the arbitrator process. The chequered lines indicate the linkage between buffer processes and their respective acceptance tests; the test must be passed before the results may be promulgated. The remaining lines indicate the linkages necessary to initiate and control the two-phase acceptance tests.

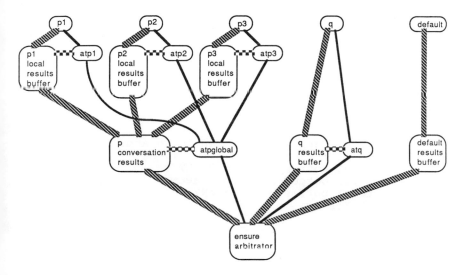

Fig.8.1 Interprocess channel linkage

8.3.4.4 Implementation of the conversation mechanism

The concurrent implementation of the conversation error detection and recovery mechanism described in Sections 8.3.4.1 - 8.3.4.3 comprises an implicit recovery line process; local results buffers and acceptance tests; a global results buffer and acceptance test; and an arbitrator process. The conversation scheme will be implemented properly only if these processes are controlled and co-ordinated such that the ensure notation is implemented correctly and without deadlock.

The principal concern in the design and implementation of the conversation is the inter-process communications which sequence and synchronise the commands governing the flow of data, the acceptance tests, the results arbitration process, and the output of an acceptable result. If these interprocess communications are constructed improperly, then they will deadlock.

The following descriptions outline the design and implementation of a conversation. Designs are presented for the local results buffer and acceptance test, (atp1, p1_buffer), the conversation results buffer and the global acceptance test, (p_conversation_buffer, atpglobal), and the arbitration process (arbitrator). Particular emphasis is placed on the description of the interaction between these processes. The complete design has been verified using Petri net techniques and is free from deadlock.

The local results buffer, p1_buffer , buffers results from process p1 pending the local acceptance test atp1.

```
PROC p1_buffer =
  SEQ
    ... get results from p1
    atp1_request ? ANY
    ... send appropriate results to atp1
    ALT          -- acceptability switch
      to_p1_buffer_request ? ANY
        ... output data to conversation buffer
      to_p1_buffer_abort ? ANY
        SKIP
  :
```

The local acceptance test atp1 is initiated on completion of p1. It obtains appropriate results from p1_buffer, tests the results for acceptability and then signals its results to the global acceptance test process.

```
PROC atp1 =
  SEQ
    ... get p1 initiation command
    atp1_request ! ANY
    ... obtain results from p1_buffer
    ... test results for acceptability
    IF
      acceptable
        to_atpglobal_accept_p[1] ! ANY
      NOT acceptable
        to_atpglobal_not_accept_p[1] ! ANY
  :
```

The conversation-buffer process, on command from the global acceptance test, signals the local buffer processes (p1_buffer, etc) to send results. It then relays appropriate results to the global acceptance test, atpglobal, and awaits commands from the arbitrator (indicating acceptability) before promulgating data to the arbitrator for further use.

```
PROC p_conversation_buffer =
  SEQ
    obtain_data ? ANY                    -- command from atpglobal
    PAR
      ... get results from p1_buffer
      ... get results from p2_buffer
      ... get results from p3_buffer
    atpglobal_request ? ANY
    ... send appropriate results to atpglobal
    ALT                                  -- acceptability switch
      p_global_request ? ANY
        ... send data to arbitrator
      p_global_abort ? ANY
        SKIP
```

The global acceptance test, atpglobal, receives the results of the local acceptance tests from each constituent test-line process in the conversation. If all are satisfactory, it commands the conversation buffer to assemble global results from the local results buffers. Atpglobal then takes relevant data from the conversation buffer to test for global acceptability. The process signals its verdict to the arbitrator process. The use of the parallel ALT statements does not impose timing constraints on the processes p1, p2 and p3 nor on the execution of their acceptance tests.

```
PROC atpglobal =
  VAR acceptable[3], local_acceptable, global_acceptable :
  SEQ
    global_acceptable := FALSE
    PAR i = [1 FOR 3]      -- input local acceptance test
                           -- results from atp1, atp2, atp3
      ALT
        to_atpglobal_accept_p[i] ? ANY
          acceptable[i] := TRUE
        to_atpglobal_not_accept_p[i] ? ANY
          acceptable[i] := FALSE
    local_acceptable := acceptable[1]
                           AND acceptable[2] AND acceptable[3]
    IF
      local_acceptable
        SEQ
          obtain_data ! ANY   -- instruct conversation
                              -- buffer to obtain data
          atpglobal_request ! ANY
          ...obtain appropriate results from conversation
                                             buffer
          ... compute acceptability of global test results
          ... (set global_acceptable)
      NOT local_acceptable
        global_acceptable := FALSE
    IF
      global_acceptable
        to_arbitrator_use_p ! ANY
      NOT global_acceptable
        to_arbitrator_not_use_p ! ANY
  :
```

The arbitrator   process, which arbitrates between the competing conversations, is implemented using nested ALTs guarded by communications from these conversations. It is this process which implements the sequence of acceptance testing implied in the ensure   notation and provides the synchronous exit to the conversation. This process also signals unsuccessful processes to abort.

```
PROC arbitrator =            -- arbitrate according to
                             -- ensure notation
  ALT
    to_arbitrator_use_p ? ANY    -- atpglobal -> acceptable
    PAR                          -- use P results; abort Q, default
      SEQ
        p_global_request ! ANY
        ... obtain P results (from p_conversation_buffer)
        q_results_abort ! ANY    -- abort q_results_buffer
        def_results_abort ! ANY -- abort
                                 -- default_results_buffer
    to_arbitrator_not_use_p ? ANY -- atpglobal ->
                                 --            unacceptable
    PAR
      p_global_abort ! ANY -- abort p conversation buffer
        ALT
          to_arbitrator_use_q ? ANY   -- atq -> acceptable
          PAR
            q_request ! ANY           -- get results from q
            ... obtain data from q
            def_results_abort ! ANY   -- abort default
          to_arbitrator_not_use_q ? ANY   -- atq ->
                                          -- unacceptable
          PAR
            def_request ! ANY
            ... obtain results from default
            q_results_abort ! ANY -- abort
                                  -- qresultsbuffer
:
```

8.4 FAULT TOLERANCE IN REAL TIME SYSTEMS

8.4.1 Real-Time Processes

8.4.1.1 Time critical processes

An application is said to be 'time-critical' if it must perform activities and produce responses at times dictated by an external environment. Typically in real-time control, a precise time-window is specified during which sensors must be sampled, a satisfactory control response computed and values output to actuators. This schedule may re-occur periodically, or be initiated at irregular intervals by stimuli from the external system. Failure to perform the required functions in time is a fault; this may lead to system failure and may be hazardous.

The software for a time-critical application will comprise processes which must be properly synchronised with each other and with the external system. Synchronism with the external system is usually imposed by a 'real-time clock' driven schedule; these times will not be dictated by the optimum use of computing resources. To ensure that component processes do not overrun, it is common to place critical timing requirements on software execution and to provide a 'time-out' mechanism to warn of timing violations.

8.4.1.2   Timeout mechanisms

It is conventional to monitor the performance of a time-critical application process [32]. Traditionally, this is done using a real-time time-lapse counter built from external circuitry. The counter is preset to trip after a pre-determined time and is initiated to run concurrently with the time-critical process. The first process to complete causes the other to abort. The mechanism is known as a 'watch-dog' timer.

If the application process has been properly designed, it will produce results well before the maximum allowed time and the 'watch-dog' timer will be aborted. A 'watch-dog' timer trip indicates the presence of a fault (which may be a software design fault or a transient or permanent malfunction of the system) and appropriate fault recovery activities should be invoked. It is therefore necessary to set the pre-determined trip period to somewhat less than the time-critical time so that fault recovery can take place and the system can still provide a timely and satisfactory response.

8.4.2   Sequential Real-time Systems

8.4.2.1   Timeout designs for sequential systems

The required timing performance can be incorporated naturally into the notation for fault tolerance introduced in Section 8.3.2.1. The time-critical construct shown below [33] is designed to produce results which are both acceptable and timely:

```
ensure acceptance test AT
   within time t
      by primary process P
      else by default process;
```

The application process P may be a simple process, a recovery block or a conversation. The timing (or performance) requirements of P, and the default actions to be taken in the event of P failing, should be detailed in the system specification. The notation does not constrain the implementation of the watchdog mechanism, nor the order in which the processes are executed.

Several strategies have been proposed for the sequential implementation of watchdog timers [33,34]. Most require the use of a centralised scheduler which ensures that either process P or the default process completes before the deadline. It is usual for the process P to be executed first, although default-first algorithms have been implemented. The default-first strategy has the advantage of ensuring the availability of acceptable results, before attempting P. However, this strategy can also be regarded as wasteful on computer resources, since more often than not the default results will be discarded as P completes successfully. In practice, the whole recovery block will itself be encompassed within a more detailed real-time schedule and the decision on which approach to adopt is often based on the desire to make efficient use of slack time for non-time-critical processing, rather than on the grounds of higher reliability.

In the P-first method, the process P should be designed to produce results which satisfy the acceptance test well within the time 't', the maximum acceptable time. The default process should be designed to produce results which are acceptable; these results must be produced, without fail, within time t_d, where $t_d < t$. The watchdog timer is used to localise the fault to the primary process, and will be set to t-t_d. If process P fails to produce acceptable results within the period t-t_d, the watchdog timer will trip and the default process, which is guaranteed to succeed, will be invoked. This method makes the common assumption that the watchdog timer, the acceptance test mechanism, and the default process are immune to faults.

Care must be exercised in the design of the watchdog timer, particularly in applications which have implications for safety, where the form of watchdog may be prescribed by the relevant codes of practice. It is common practice to configure the watchdog timer to raise an external interrupt which interrupts the processor and causes the scheduler to abort the timed-out process P. However, the use of this technique results in a non-deterministic design. An alternative deterministic approach requires the process P to poll the timer to confirm that the timeout has not elapsed. This method assumes that P remains active; it cannot cope with the class of fault which causes P to hang.

8.4.3 Concurrent Real-time Systems

8.4.3.1 Timeout mechanisms for concurrent systems

A concurrent timeout mechanism can be designed [35] in which the watchdog timer is initiated and executed in parallel with both the primary and default processes as shown below:

```
PAR
  P
  timer
  default
```

The basis of the design is the formulation of an asynchronous race between P and 'timer'. The Occam PAR construct provides the means of initiating the race and the Occam ALT can be used to terminate the race provided the design incorporates a mechanism for absorbing outstanding interprocess communications when the ALT terminates.

The process 'timer' is a deterministic Occam process which is capable of protecting specific sets of processes or communication constructs. (Occam does not support interrupts in the conventional fashion).

The nucleus of the watchdog timer process, timer, is:

```
DEF timeoutvalue = 100; -- as appropriate
VAR starttime:
SEQ
   TIME ? starttime
   TIME ? AFTER starttime + timeoutvalue
   timertrip ! ANY:
```

This form of timer can be user to provide protection for a time critical process and to monitor time critical inputs in order to avoid overlong process suspension.

Considerable care is required in the detailed design of a concurrent timeout mechanism if the design is to be deterministic and free from deadlock. It is assumed that the default process will produce acceptable and timely results without fail. However, process P may fail to provide acceptable results within the deadline defined by the timer. In particular, the following cases must be accommodated without fault or deadlock:

P completes first : the timer should be aborted (to prevent it initiating unsatisfiable communications) and the results from P should be used in the acceptance test.

P and timer complete simultaneously : the results from P should be used in the acceptance test.

(In both cases, if the results are unacceptable, then the default results should be used).

Timer completes first : process P has failed. It is necessary to design for two possible scenario:

Process P is 'late' but still active : P should be aborted to prevent it attempting to communicate with other processes, and the default results should be used.

The fault in P is such that it can no longer respond, even to those communications commanding it to abort : the design should ensure that the system can operate satisfactorily using the default process and that when the inevitable deadlock occurs (since the initiating PAR will never terminate) its external effects are minimised.

Therefore, it is important to design the watchdog timer process and the primary process P to be as responsive as possible to interprocess messages which would command each process to abort. This can be achieved by partitioning P into small blocks of code which are interleaved with a 'scan' of the timeout communication channel. If the timeout has tripped, the computation is terminated, otherwise P runs to completion. This can be implemented by a prioritised ALT where timer stimulates the guard at highest priority and the process which computes the next phase of results is guarded at a lower priority by SKIP (which is always ready) .

8.4.3.2 Deadlock-free timeout designs for concurrent systems

The concurrent timeout mechanism of Section 8.4.3.1 can be implemented as three concurrent processes P, timer, and default , which are initiated in parallel by a centralised co-ordinating process which also handles process termination. Process P and the timer race against each other. The outcome of the race is communicated to the co-ordinating process which then aborts the losing process.

The co-ordinating process incorporates two parallel subprocesses to handle process termination and abortion. One subprocess is activated primarily by the completion of P and will abort the timer; the other is activated primarily by a timeout trip and aborts P. Both subprocesses are guaranteed to run to completion because the inactive subprocess is activated by the process which aborts. Thus, subprocess (A) is activated by either the timer tripping or the timer being aborted on the completion of P. Similarly, subprocess (B) is activated by either P completing or P being aborted on timeout. This mechanism is implemented by the dual use of channels which switch roles between command or acknowledgement signals. This 'cross-coupled' structure is characteristic of such deadlock-free designs.

The design is completed by introducing a buffer process for collecting appropriate results for acceptance testing and onward propagation. This 'result buffer' process must, of course, absorb outputs from both subprocesses (A) and (B).

```
PROC P =
  VAR exit, status:
  SEQ
    -- initialisation
    exit := FALSE
    status := noabort
    WHILE NOT exit
      SEQ
        PRI ALT
          Pabort ? ANY
            SEQ
              status := abort
              exit := TRUE
              Pcomplete ! abort
          SKIP
            -- compute partial results
    IF
      status = noabort
        SEQ
          Pcomplete ! noabort
          Pabort ? ANY
          Prequest ? ANY
          -- send results to results buffer
          Pdata ! -- data --
      status = abort
        SKIP:


PROC timer =
  VAR clock:
  SEQ
    TIME ? clock
    ALT
      timerabort ? ANY
        timertrip ! notrip
      TIME ? AFTER clock + timeout
        SEQ
          timertrip ! trip
          timerabort ? ANY:


PROC resultbuffer
  -- not illustrated


PROC default
  -- not illustrated
```

```
-- the co-ordinating process
  PAR
    P
    timer
    default
    resultbuffer
    SEQ            -- (A)
      timertrip ? status1
      toresultbuffer1 ! status1
      Pabort ! ANY
    SEQ            -- (B)
      Pcomplete ? status2
      toresultbuffer2 ! status2
      timerabort ! ANY:
```

This method provides protection against a time-critical process overrunning its allowed execution time. As in all methods which check the state of a timer process, the protected process must be partitioned into finely grained sections of code which are interleaved with checks on the state of the timer. Within these sections of code the protected process is unresponsive to the watchdog timer. However, once the timeout signal has been accepted by the protected process, the default process can take over and housekeeping operations associated with the aborted process can proceed in parallel.

Petri net analysis shows that this design is free from deadlock [35] . The design provides timeout protection except for the case in which process P hangs. Since P can not be terminated in these circumstances, the encompassing PAR construct will fail. Some protection can be offered if the design ensures that other processes are unaffected by the failure of P so that the system can continue to operate satisfactorily using the default process. The deadlock within the PAR construct will become perceptible when the software is required to terminate; if it can be arranged that this takes place only after all critical operations have taken place, then the failure is not likely to be dangerous.

8.4.3.3 The protection of communications

Software fault tolerance techniques for concurrent real-time systems can also be used to protect the interprocess communications which ensure the proper synchronisation and operation of the distributed systems [5,36]. This is particularly important because these systems depend on the integrity of the inter-process communications.

In practice, the communications medium may not be immune to faults and must be regarded as a potential source of errors. Typical errors are erroneous messages or messages which fail to arrive. In synchronous systems, these errors will manifest themselves as erroneous messages, which can be detected by acceptance testing, or by the failure to exchange a message across a particular channel even though both participants are ready. Prompt recognition of such a fault is essential if recovery actions are to be initiated within a critical time period and deadlock avoided.

Communication transactions can be protected using watchdog timers only if there is a logical pairing of the protective mechanisms on each side of the transaction. For example, if a timeout is used on the receive primitive only, the sending process will hang if the timeout operates, since the sending process has no means of determining whether the communication medium has failed. A logically paired timeout cannot be placed on the sending process without using an output guard; this requires an extension to conventional concurrent programming languages. This problem is generic to attempts to protect a communication at the primitive or transaction level.

A solution can be obtained by decreasing the level of granularity at which protection is applied, by enclosing a communication which must be protected within a conversation. One property of the conversation is the absence of communications through the sidewalls. Therefore, it is possible to protect the conversation using a watchdog timer which monitors the performance of the complete set of processes and communication transactions within the conversation. In the event of a participating process becoming unresponsive, or a failure in the communications between processes, the conversation will not terminate. The default process or conversation will then be invoked by the timer and the failure need only become perceptible after other time-critical processes succeed in producing results.

8.5 CONCLUSIONS

Software fault tolerance techniques for sequential and concurrent real-time systems, such as recovery blocks, conversation schemes and concurrent watchdog mechanisms, can be used to protect specific processes and functions. They can also be used to protect the interprocess communications which ensure the proper synchronisation and operation of the distributed systems.

Many of these techniques have been proved in practice. The newer concurrent techniques will undoubtedly prove useful in the design of robust concurrent systems, such as real-time control systems. The need for these techniques will grow due to the sophistication of the logical structures, and the subtlety of the bugs, in advanced concurrent real-time systems.

REFERENCES

1. INMOS, 1984, "occam programming manual", Prentice Hall.

2. INMOS, 1985, "IMS T414 Reference Manual".

3. May,D.,1983, "occam", Sigplan Notices, vol 18, no 4, pp. 67-79.

4. Hoare, C.A.R., 1985, "Communicating sequential processes," Prentice Hall.

5. Kramer,J., Magee, J. and Sloman, M., 1981, "Intertask communication primitives for distributed computer control systems", Proc 2nd Int Conf. on 'Distributed Computer Systems', Paris, pp. 404 - 411.

6. Ceri, S. and Pelagatti, G., 1984, "Distributed database principles and systems", McGraw-Hill.

7. Gray, J.N., 1978, "Notes on database operating systems", Lecture notes in Computer Science, Vol. 60, Springer Verlag, pp. 393-481.

8. Hill, M.R., 1987, "New techniques for fault tolerant software in distributed real-time control systems", EEEAP Technical Report, Aston University.

9. Peterson, J.L., 1981, "Petri net theory and the modeling of systems", Prentice Hall.

10. Mekly, L.J. and Yau, S.S., 1980, "Software design representation using abstract process networks", IEEE Trans. Software Engineering, SE-6, pp.420-434.

11. Carpenter. G.F., 1987, " The use of occam and Petri Nets in the simulation of logic structures for the control of loosely coupled distributed systems", Proc. UKSC Conference on Computer Simulation, (UKSC 1987), pp. 30-35.

12. Hoare, C.A.R., 1981, "A calculus of total correctness for communicating processes", Oxford University Programming Research Group Monograph 23, Oxford Press.

13. "Software Tools for Application to Large Real-time Systems", 1984, The STARTS Guide, Department of Trade & Industry, U.K.

14. Neumann, P.G., 1985, "Some computer related disasters and other egregious horrors", A.C.M. SIGSOFT Software Engineering Notes, Vol.10, No.1, pp. 6-11.

15. Musa,J.D., Iannino,A. and Okumoto,K., 1987, "Software reliability" McGraw Hill.

16. Avienzis, A., 1985, "The N version approach to fault tolerant software", IEEE Trans SE., Vol. SE-11, No.12, pp. 1491-1501.

17. Hecht, H., 1979, "Fault tolerant software", IEEE Trans. on Reliability, Vol. R-28, pp. 227-232.

18. Anderson, T., and Lee, P.A., 1981, "Fault Tolerance, Principles and Practice", Prentice Hall.

19. Anderson, T.(ed), 1987, "Resilient Computing Systems", Collins Professional and Technical Books.

20. Levenson,N.G., 1983, "Software Fault Tolerance; the case for forward error recovery", Proc AIAA Conf on Computers in Aerospace, pp. 50-54.

21. Campbell, R.H., and Randell, B., 1986, "Error recovery in asynchronous systems" IEEE Trans. Software Engineering, Vol. SE-12, pp. 811-826.

22. Horning, J.J., Lauer, H.C., Melliar-Smith, P.M. and Randell,B., 1974, "A program structure for error detection and recovery" in Lecture Notes in Computer Science, Vol 16, Springer Verlag, pp. 171-187.

23. Randell, B., 1975, "System structure for software fault tolerance", IEEE Trans. SE., Vol SE-1, pp. 220-232.

24. Knight, J.C., and Levenson, N.G., 1986, "An empirical study of failure probability in multi-version software", Proc. 16th Int. Symposium on Fault Tolerant Computing Systems,pp. 165-170.

25. Jackson, P.R., and White, B.A., 1983, "The application of fault tolerant techniques to a real-time system", Proc. Int. Conf. on Safety of Computer Control Systems, (Safecomp '83), pp. 75-82.

26. Merlin, P.M., and Randell, B., 1978, "State restoration in distributed systems", Proc 8th Int. Symp. on Fault Tolerant Computers, pp. 129-134.

27. Russell, D.L., 1980, "State restoration in systems of communicating processes", IEEE Trans. Software Engineering, Vol SE-6, pp. 183-194.

28. Campbell, R.H., Anderson,T., and Randell,B., 1983, "Practical fault tolerant software for asynchronous systems", Proc. Int. Conf. on Safety of Computer Control Systems (Safecomp '83), pp. 59-65.

29. Gregory, S.T. and Knight, J.C., 1985, "A new linguistic approach to background error recovery", Proc. 15th Int. Symp. on Fault Tolerant Computing", pp. 404 - 409.

30. Tyrrell, A.M. and Holding, D.J., 1986, "Design of reliable software in distributed systems using the conversation scheme", IEEE Trans on Software Engineering, Vol. SE-12, pp. 921-928.

31. Carpenter, G.F., Holding, D.J., and Tyrrell, A.M., 1987, "The design and simulation of software fault tolerant mechanisms for application in distributed processing systems" Microprocessing and Microprogramming, Vol. 22, in press.

32. Hecht, H., 1976, "Fault tolerant software for real-time applications", Computing Surveys, Vol.8, No.4, pp.391-407.

33. Campbell, R.H., Horton, K. and Belford, G.G, 1979, "Simulations of a fault tolerant deadline mechanism" in Digest of papers, Fault Tolerant Computing Systems, Madison, pp. 95-101.

34. Upadhyaya, J.S. and Saluja, K.K, 1986, "A watchdog processor based general roll back technique with multiple retries", IEEE Trans Software Engineering, Vol. SE-12, pp. 87-95.

35. Carpenter,G.F., Holding, D.J, and Tyrrell, A.M., 1987, "Analysis and protection of interprocess communications in real-time systems", Software Engineering for Real-Time Systems , (IERE London 1987) pp. 135-143.

36. Holding, D.J, Carpenter, G.F, and Tyrrell, A.M, 1984, "Aspects of software engineering for systems with safety implications", Proc 6th IEEE/Eurel Conf on Computers in communications and control (Eurocon 84), Brighton, England, pp. 235-239.

Chapter 9

PWM inverter control using the INMOS transputer

M. Sumner & Dr. G.M. Asher

9.1 INTRODUCTION

Field Orientated or vector control of A.C. Induction motors is a recent technique in which the speed and torque of the cheap and reliable A.C. induction motor is controlled with superior dynamic performance to the more costly and unreliable D.C.machine. The principle behind the vector control strategy is described in Chapter 7. The strategy demands considerable real-time signal processing and as such full microprocessor implementations require the use of multiprocessors [1,2,3]. The innate concurrency of the transputer was thus felt to be highly suitable for this application. After an initial exchange of ideas with UCNW Bangor, a project aimed at constructing a transputer-controlled high-performance induction motor test bed at the Dept. of Electrical and Electronic Engineering, University of Nottingham was started in October 1986.

This Chapter describes our initial experiences with the transputer in achieving as a first stage, a user- interactive open-loop controller for the induction motor drive. A single T414 was found to be adequate for the purposes of timing/synchronisation, host interaction and the real-time generation of "pulse width modulated" (PWM) waveforms required for the drive's power electronics. The transputer algorithms have been implemented and good open-loop control of the drive rig has been achieved. The work is on-going and we plan to add a further transputer in order to implement the closed-loop vector control. Indeed, the addition of transputers in modular fashion allows for the development of an induction motor drive rig having a considerable real-time processing capability. We plan to exploit this capability for researching advanced control strategies and global parameter estimation techniques for the drive system.

9.2 DRIVE SYSTEM OVERVIEW

Speed control of an A.C. motor is achieved by varying the applied frequency of excitation. This is achieved by a power electronic converter, the type used (for all but very high power drives) being shown in Fig.9.1. The mains voltage is 3-phase rectified and smoothed. The D.C. voltage is then converted to 3-phase variable frequency A.C. by an inverter of six power transistors which are switched to construct a 'sinusoidal' waveform out of continuously varying pulse widths as shown in Fig.9.2.

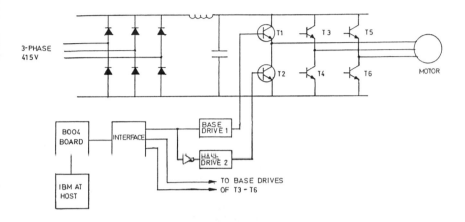

Fig.9.1. Speed control of an A.C. motor using a power electronic converter

Fig.9.2. 'Sinusoidal' waveform composed of continuously varying pulse widths

    The base drives to the transistors are pulse width modulated (PWM) waveforms and, in this work, these controlled pwm signals are generated by the transputer. The rate at which the transistors are switched determines the excitation frequency whilst the relative pulse widths within a cycle determine the magnitude of the motor voltage. For vector control the magnitude, frequency and phase (the position within the cycle at any instant in time) are all independent control variables affecting the pwm generation process. For open loop control, as hitherto implemented, phase control is redundant whilst a constraint on correct motor operation is that applied voltage is made proportional to frequency in order to achieve full flux levels inside the machine. The motor voltage vs. frequency characteristic is shown in Fig.9.3.

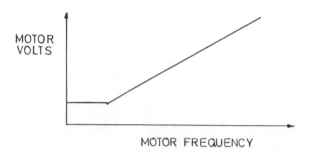

Fig.9.3. Motor voltage vs. frequency characteristic

At low frequency the motor winding resistance becomes significant, resulting in a voltage 'boost' being required. At higher frequencies, it may be necessary to operate in a quasi square-wave mode in order to provide the full flux levels. In this region of operation pulses are 'dropped' as detailed in the next Section.

Further practical constraints on the generalized pwm waveform derive from the protection of the inverter's transistors. With reference to Fig.9.1, transistors T1 and T2 must never be ON at the same time. Since their base signals are mutual inverses, a 'lockout' time (20μs for this project) is introduced between the falling edge (turn off) of one transistor and the turn on of the other. A minimum pulse time of 20μs is also introduced in order to allow snubber recovery upon switching. The minimum pulse time check is incorporated into the transputer pwm generator algorithm whilst the lock-out protection is delegated to the transputer-inverter interface.

The motor used is a 380V, 5HP, 6-pole induction motor with a wound rotor for experimental flexibility. The power converter has been provided by Control Techniques plc of Newtown, Powys.

9.3 PWM WAVEFORM GENERATION STRATEGY

The PWM calculation strategy, implemented on the transputer, was one of 'approximate' natural sampling. The pwm signal was controlled as a three-phase pulse train, the width of the pulses being generated by the comparison of a three-phase sinewave (the modulation wave) of variable amplitude, phase, and frequency for vector control, and a fixed amplitude triangular wave (carrier wave). The basic principle is illustrated in Fig.9.4.

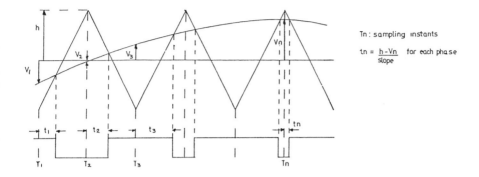

Fig.9.4. PWM waveform generation

At each sampling instant, n, the time until the next crossing point of the carrier and modulation waves, t_n, can be approximated by

$$t_n = \frac{h - V\sin(\omega_m t + \theta)}{slope}$$

where

V = modulation amplitude (corresponding to motor volts)
ω_m = modulation frequency (corresponding to motor speed)
θ = phase (redundant for open-loop control)
h = carrier amplitude (set at unity)
slope = slope of carrier, and
t = time at sampling instant.

The modulation index of this system is defined as the ratio of modulation wave amplitude to carrierwave amplitude. Therefore, when the modulation index becomes greater than unity, it can be seen that there will be a requirement to 'pulsedrop', i.e. set the length of the pulses at the peak of the modulation wave to a value greater than the half carrier period. Fig.9.5 illustrates the output waveshape in this 'quasi' square-wave mode. This mode of operation is necessary to give the required voltage output at higher frequencies, but does lead to increased harmonics in the pwm signal.

Fig.9.5. Output waveshape in 'quasi' square-wave mode

The choice of carrierwave was influenced by several factors. A high ratio of carrier frequency to modulation frequency was desirable in order to improve the accuracy of the approximation and reduce the modulation frequency related harmonics of the system. These harmonics are responsible for most of the system losses. A high carrier frequency also enables a fast response to changes in the system parameters: an important requirement for vector controlled drives. Furthermore, a high carrier frequency results in a reduction of the carrier frequency related harmonics in the motor current, due to the large inherent inductance of the drive.

A synchronous system, whereby carrierwave and modulation signals are always in phase, was also desirable. Asynchronism, the use of a constant frequency carrier wave may result in small beating effects in the motor speed and current when running at high speed. Additionally, transistor switching losses become more significant at low speeds as do the voltage loss effects due to the lockout circuit. However the use of an asynchronous carrierwave simplified the carrierwave routine, and allowed for a more straightforward development of the pwm program. It also simplified the design of the hardware interface circuit by keeping the range of the count values constant.

Thus a constant carrier frequency was chosen and its value could be preset to 2 or 4 KHz. The development of a synchronous carrier was to be pursued at a later date.

9.4 THE TRANSPUTER SYSTEM

An INMOS B004 Transputer Evaluation Board [4] was used, mounted within an IBM PC compatible host machine. The B004 board contains one T414 32 bit transputer with 2 kbytes of on-chip RAM, 2Mbytes of external DRAM, and an interface for communication with the host machine. The transputer itself operates at 10 MIPS. It communicates with the host using one of its four serial communication links, via an INMOS C002 Link Adapter [5] which converts serial information into byte wide parallel information and vice versa. The remaining three links may be used for communication with other transputers, or further link adapters. The links operate at a nominal 10 Mbits/second.

Transputer programs were developed using the Transputer Development System [6] - a software package run on the host machine. The language used was OCCAM1, a high level language produced specifically for the transputer, which allowed the user to design and configure a system comprised of parallel processes. The recently introduced OCCAM2 was not available at the commencement of the work. Although an OCCAM2 implementation is expected to simplify some procedures it is noted that real-time processing constraints demand the use of scaled integer arithmetic. OCCAM1 is still considered to be sufficient in this respect.

The PWM generator routine produced for this system ran on a single transputer so that the parallel processes are implemented in a user transparent time slicing. The routine allowed for information to be input from the host machine's keyboard and subsequently generates values corresponding to the pulsewidths of the required three-phase pwm signal. These values were then output using two of the transputer's serial links.

The interface unit was a custom-built circuit to convert the information output from the transputer into the required control signals for the inverter.

9.5 SOFTWARE STRUCTURES

The overall occam software structure is illustrated in Fig.9.6. and the pseudo-code is given in Appendix 9.1.

As shown, the system comprises of a set-up routine followed by three parallel routines run on a single transputer. A fourth routine is run concurrently on the host processor. Parallelism on a single transputer is achieved using a timeslicing technique and processes communicate with each other using predefined software channels. Communication between the host and the transputer is achieved using one of the transputer's links.

9.5.1 Set-Up Routine

The set-up routine is listed in Appendix 9.2. Firstly it receives a value from the host routine which defines whether the system will run with a carrier frequency of 2 or 4 kHz, and subsequently defines the system constants. Secondly the initial values for the system variables are set to ensure a correct and predictable startup.

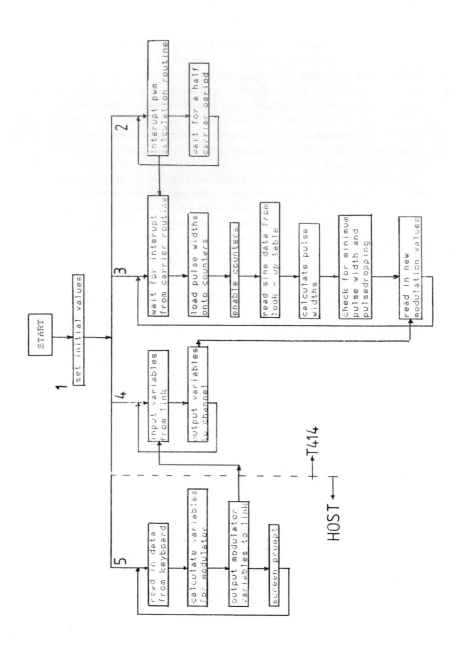

Fig.9.6 Software structure

Finally, the hardware counters are programmed for the correct mode of operation and initially cleared. Link1 passes data from the program and presents it via link adapter 1 to the data input registers of the counter/timer chip. Link 2 is used to address the correct counter and provide read/write and enable signals.

9.5.2 Carrierwave Routine

The listing for the carrierwave routine is shown in Appendix 9.3.

This process is introduced using the PRI PAR statement and as such runs using the 1μs high priority timer. It should be noted that only one parallel routine may access this timer when running on a single transputer. The process inputs the current value of the clock using the TIME ?(now) statement and then waits for a half carrier period using the TIME ?AFTER(now + step) statement. On completion of the timeout this process sends an interrupt to the pwm calculation routine via the software channel interrupt1. The value passed along this channel alternates between campm and campp corresponding to the peak or trough of the carrierwave. This value is read into the pwm calculation routine for use in the subsequent pulsewidth calculations.

9.5.3 Main PWM Calculation Routine

The listing for this process is given in Appendix 9.4. The purpose of this process is to calculate the pulse widths on a real-time basis, using the equation outlined in Section 9.5.3. In order to provide a sufficiently fast calculation time, integer calculation must be used as real number routines prove time consuming. This necessitates the use of a memory-based sine look-up table as real-time sine calculation in this application is impossible. The sine table is generated by OCCAM real number routines and down-loaded as integer values (0 - 200) before the pwm generator is started.

The process is triggered by the interrupt from the carrierwave routine. When the carrieramp value is presented on the channel interrupt1 the calculation routine reads it in and proceeds. The first instruction requires that the present value of the low priority clock (64μs tick) is read into the variable y for use later. The pulsewidths calculated from the previous half cycle are then downloaded to the hardware counters via the two links and link adapters. This process requires the output of three values per counter and these are of a single byte length only. Consequently the BYTE.SLICE.OUTPUT instruction has been employed which allows the transfer of a sole byte across the link, and thus speeds up data transfer. The counters are enabled simultaneously once the third count value has been loaded, and it thus can be seen that the initial-ization of the timers is synchronised to the carrierwave interrupt. This results in a half carrier cycle delay between update and initialization, which can be compensated for in the vector control system.

The three phase calculation routine then follows. Three input variables govern this calculation. The first is the carrierwave amplitude read in earlier. The other two are the modulation wave amplitude Vamp, and a variable called leap which represents the angular step of the modulation wave per half cycle of the carrier wave. Leap is calculated and scaled in the update routine described later, and is used to determine the addresses required to access the sine look-up table.

The sine look-up table consists of 10000 sine values in the range 0 - 200, for 0 - 180 degrees in 0.018 degree steps. The size of this table is unusually large, but it enables a speed resolution of 0.2 Hz when running at 2 kHz carrier frequency and also provides a means for experi-mentation with harmonic elimination at a later date. The address of 0 degrees is defined by the constant baseaddr and that of 180 degrees by topaddr. For each half carrier period the address pointer count1 is incremented by leap and this value of sine is fetched. If the value of count1 exceeds the 0 - 180 degree range another pointer add1 is used to access the sine table and a toggle is used to negate the sine value. If the value of count1 exceeds the 180 - 360 degree range count1 has 19999 subtracted from it (equivalent to 360 degrees) and the modulation cycle repeats.

Once the sine values have been determined the pulse-widths can be obtained. As described earlier, the power devices on the inverter require a minimum on and off time. Also, at higher speeds the pwm signals may need to go into quasi square-wave operation. These requirements are assessed during the calculation stage. The value of the pulsewidth, calculated during the last sample period (tab1last), is used to determine whether the present pulse needs extending to conform with minimum pulse requirements. Pulsedropping is employed when the modulation factor becomes greater than unity, and a complicated checking routine using present and previous variables is used to determine at which point of the modulation cycle pulsedropping is entered and exited.

Once the three pulsewidths have been calculated the remaining part of the half carrier period can be used to update the variables Vamp and Leap. This is done using the ALT statement whereby the routine waits for either new variables to be placed on the channel update2 (connected to the transputer's update process) or a timeout. The timeout is necessary as the update of variables is not synchronised to the carrier and thus may occur just before a carrier interrupt. If this occurs the time to update delays the carrier interrupt and thus extends the sample time haphazardly.

9.5.4 The   Software Buffer

This routine is listed in Appendix 9.5 and simply reads in information from the link connected to the host processor, and transfers it via a software channel to the calculation routine. As mentioned earlier the update of variables is not synchronised to the carrier and, as such, direct reading of information from the link into the calculation routine results in serious extension of the sample period.

9.5.5 The Host's Update Routine

This routine is listed in Appendix 9.6. There are three requirements of this routine. Firstly, it is needed to drive the keyboard and screen to allow the modulation frequency to be changed and displayed. Secondly, it was necessary to provide a controlled ramp increase and decrease in frequency in response to a step change at the keyboard, at a rate of 2 Hz/second. This control was to prevent the motor from generating or drawing excessively high currents during acceleration. Finally, the routine had to control the relationship of the modulation amplitude Vamp, to the modulation frequency according to the ramp shown in Fig.9.3.

The system is initialized by typing in the required carrier frequency. This is immediately passed to the set-up routine on the transputer via the link, and the pwm generator is started. Speed settings are read in from the keyboard using the READPARAMETERS procedure which converts an ASCII character string into the corresponding integer value. A repeat statement is then used to ramp the frequency up or down accordingly. The number of iterations is determined by the change in frequency (Fnew - Fold) and for each iteration the routine employs a timeout of 64 μs. The repeat process calculates the required Vamp from the frequency by a simple constant. Low speed voltage boost is achieved using an IF statement. The value Leap is then calculated by a formula which relates the modulation and carrier frequencies to find the angular step of modulation wave per half carrier period. Once the set speed has been reached the display announces this and prompts a new setting.

9.6 TRANSPUTER - INVERTER INTERFACE

The transputer-inverter interface was designed to take the calculated pulse widths from the transputer link and convert them into the control signals required by the inverter. The block diagram is shown in Fig.9.7.

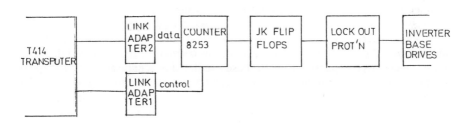

Fig.9.7. Transputer-inverter interface

The counter/timer device used was an INTEL 8253 Programmable Interval Timer [7], chosen because it contains three independent counters which can operate well at a count rate of 1 MHz. The device requires twelve separate input lines - eight bits for data and four bits for addressing and control. Thus two link adapters were used, one to activate each counter and one to present the count values. (See Fig.9.7). The counters were used in Mode 1 as this allowed new count values to be loaded whilst the old count values were being timed out.

The operation of the counters was such that whilst timing out their output was low and on completion of the count the output goes high. This necessitated the use of a JK Flip Flop on each output in order to invert every second pulse and produce the correct pwm waveforms. The non-inverted and inverted outputs from these flip flops were used as the basis for the two transistor base drive signals per phase. Lockout was introduced onto the rising edge of these six signals using the circuit shown in Fig.9.8.

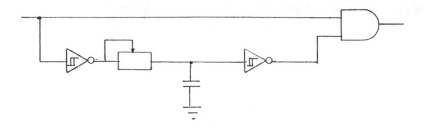

Fig.9.8 Circuit to implement lockout

These signals were then opto-isolated and stepped up from TTL to 0-15V CMOS level for use as the control inputs for the inverter.The bulk of this circuit was constructed on Veroboard, but the link adapters themselves were mounted on unetched pcb, with the copper acting as a ground plane. This was necessary due to the presence of a 200MHz internal clock within the link adapters themselves. Connection to the rest of the circuit was made using point to point wiring.

The interface circuit was thoroughly tested before connecting to the inverter and was found to work effectively. Lockout was correctly introduced and the output pwm waveforms compared well with those predicted by a naturally sampled system. It was noted that the minimum time required by the program to output a single byte to the link adapters was 5μs, using the BYTE.SLICE.OUTPUT instruction for a single byte. Nine output statements are required to load the three counters and as such the 45μs output time per sample period proves to be a significant fraction of the 4KHz sample time.

9.7 RESULTS

The transputer-based pwm strategy has been successfully tested up to motor speeds of up to 60Hz (quasi square wave operation) with carrier frequencies of both 2 and 4 KHz. Figs.9.9, 9.10, and 9.11 show the 3-phase generated pwm control signals for motor speeds of 40,50 and 60 Hz using a 2 KHz carrier frequency.

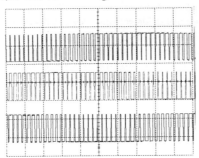

**Fig.9.9 3-Phase generated PWM control signal
40Hz, 2KHz carrier)**

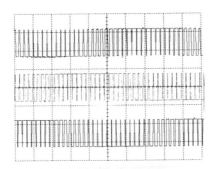

**Fig.9.10 3-Phase generated PWM control signal
(50Hz, 2KHz carrier)**

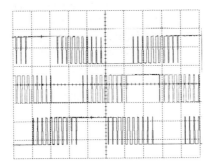

**Fig.9.11 3-Phase generated PWM control signal
(60Hz, 2KHz carrier)**

Power spectra of the pwm control signal, transistor base drive and the resultant line - line motor voltage are shown in Figs. 9.12 - 9.14 for 2 KHz carrier frequency and motor speeds of 10, 50, and 60 Hz. At low speeds the pwm and base drive signals are noticeably free of modulation frequency related harmonics, and those present in the motor line voltage are small. The second harmonic effects are due to the introduction of lock-out. At speeds greater than 40 Hz the requirement of a minimum pulse width becomes significant and increases the third, fifth, and ninth harmonic content of the pwm and base drive signals. However of these, only the fifth harmonic is significant in the motor line voltage. This is consistent with the approximate natural sampling technique employed. At speeds greater than 52 Hz the pwm generator operates in a quasi square wave mode and as a consequence the harmonic content of all these signals rises. However the motor line voltage has only a small amount of tertiary harmonics present which confirms the use of a well balanced system.

Fig.9.15 shows a graph of the motor's fundamental line voltage as a function of its frequency. The curve is consistent with that set in software, with the non-linear region of 42 - 52 Hz being attributed to the presence of the minimum pulse width requirement in this area of operation. The system was found to have a speed resolution of 0.2 Hz (at 2 KHz) and 0.4 Hz (at 4 KHz), as designed, although at speeds less than 0.5 Hz the motor was found to 'cog'.

Monitoring of the carrier frequency over the full motor speed range, both at steady state and during ramp up and down showed that it remained constant throughout. This confirmed the effectiveness of the transputer's high priority timer, and showed that the effect of timeslicing on its operation was negligible. Timing of the calculation process time was carried out by setting and resetting one of the free bits on the link adapter every sample period.

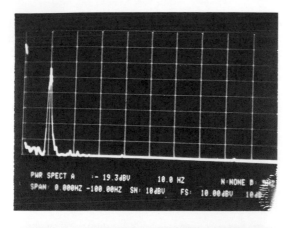

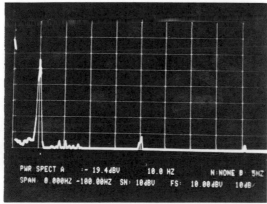

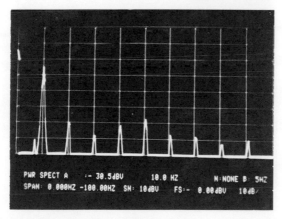

Fig.9.12 Power spectra of PWM waveform (10Hz, 2KHz carrier)
    (a) Pre-Lockout;
    (b) Transistor base drive;
    (c) Motor line voltage

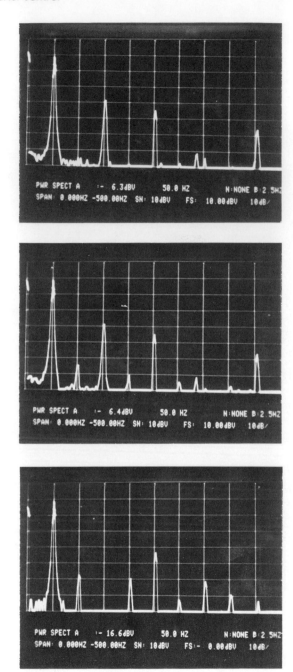

Fig.9.13 Power spectra of PWM waveform (50Hz, 2KHz carrier)
   (a) Pre-Lockout;
   (b) Transistor base drive;
   (c) Motor line voltage

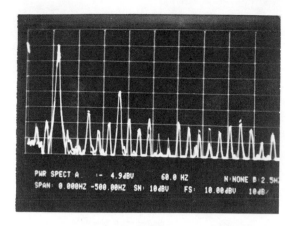

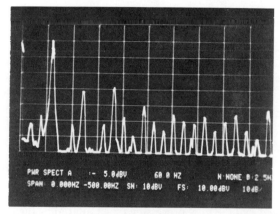

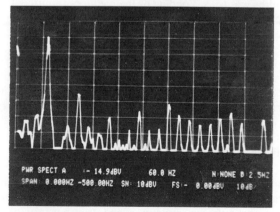

Fig.9.14 Power spectra of PWM waveform (60Hz, 2KHz carrier)
(a) Pre-Lockout;
(b) Transistor base drive;
(c) Motor line voltage

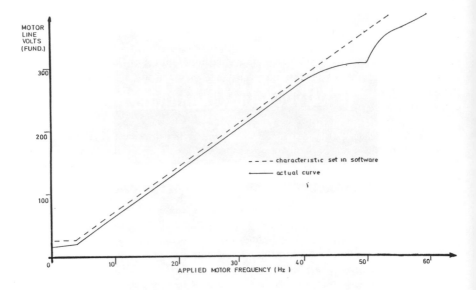

Fig.9.15 Motor line voltage vs. Applied motor frequency

This showed that the total processing time required by the calculation of the 3-phase pulse widths was 65μs. Loading of the counters required 45μs and thus the total calculation run-time was just shorter than the 125μs sample time of the 4 Khz system.

The performance of the transputer-based pwm system proved to be extremely reliable. The inverter and motor were driven smoothly and consistently over the full frequency range. However it must be noted that only no-load tests have been carried out and the operation of the inverter was maintained well within its rating.

9.8 CONCLUSIONS AND FUTURE DEVELOPMENTS

The capability of a single transputer for providing user interactive pwm waveform generation with real-time pulse-width calculation has been demonstrated. The simplicity of the software structures and transparency of the transputer architecture has led to a fast system development time - a significant advantage over conventional microprocessor programming systems. At present the main restriction on the program execution time is the time taken to input and output using the links and link adapters. This limits the maximum carrier frequency of the system to 4 KHz, although at present this frequency is regarded as a maximum due to the capabilities of the inverter's switching elements.

A second transputer can now be added to perform the vector control processing for closed-loop drive operation. Implementation of the control strategy as occam routines should be straightforward, and major problems foreseen concern the input of the feedback signals. As the control routine will be synchronised to the carrier routine no problems are predicted with inter-transputer communications.

It is envisaged that a synchronous pwm generator will be implemented whereby the carrier frequency is controlled as a function of the modulation frequency. The main restriction with this system will arise from the counter/timer circuit used, as this governs the maximum count time.

Further transputers will be employed to meet the processing requirements of future research work. Initially, system monitoring will be developed to allow parameters to be stored prior to fault and provide a means for fault diagnosis. Such a system could also provide displays to simulate transient responses within the motor. Rotor parameter identification will also be developed, and this will lead to the production of an 'adaptive' system of control, whereby the effects of temperature and frequency on the motor can be compensated.

REFERENCES

1.Gabriel,R., Leonhard,W. and C.Nordby,C., 1980, "Field Orientated Control of a Standard AC Motor using Microprocessors", IEEE Trans. Ind. Appl., vol.IA-16, pp.186-192.

2. Harashima,F., Kondo,S., Kajita,M. and Susono,M., 1985, "Multimicroprocessor Based System For a Quick Response Induction Motor Drive", IEEE Trans. Ind. Appl., vol.IA-21, pp.602-609.

3. Kubo,K., Watanabe,M., Ohmae,T., Kamiyama,K., 1985, "A Fully Digitised Speed Regulator using Multimicroprocessor System for Induction Motor Drives" IEEE Trans.Ind. Appl., vol.IA-21, pp.1001-1067.

4. Ghee,S., "IMS B004 IBM PC add in board", INMOS Technical Note 11.

5. IMS C002 link adapter, INMOS Data Sheet.

6. IMS D700 User Manual, INMOS Publication.

7. 8253/8253-5 Programmable Interval Timer, INTEL Data Sheet.

APPENDIX 9.1

Pseudo - Code For PWM Generator

```
... declare variables
... declare channels
... declare constants

SEQ
   ... set up process

  -- pwm generator
  PRI PAR
     ... carrierwave process
     PAR
        ... pulsewidth calculation process
        ... update process (software buffer)
```

APPENDIX 9.2

Set Up Process

```
SEQ
  -- clear counter 1
  BYTE.SLICE.OUTPUT(link1,d,8,2)    -- prep wr mode word
  BYTE.SLICE.OUTPUT(link2,d,0,2)    -- mode word
  BYTE.SLICE.OUTPUT(link1,d,10,2)   -- wr mode word
  BYTE.SLICE.OUTPUT(link1,d,20,2)   -- prep wr counter 1
  BYTE.SLICE.OUTPUT(link2,d,6,2)    -- count := #0000
  BYTE.SLICE.OUTPUT(link1,d,6,2)    -- wr count
  ... clear counter 2
  ... clear counter 3
  -- load mode onto counter 1
  BYTE.SLICE.OUTPUT(link1,b,0,2)    -- prep wr mode word
  BYTE.SLICE.OUTPUT(link2,a,6,2)    -- mode word
  BYTE.SLICE.OUTPUT(link1,b,2,2)    -- wr mode word
  ... mode to counter 2
  ... mode to counter 3

  -- set variables according to fc
  update1 ? fc
  IF
    fc = 2
      SEQ
        tc := 250
        step := 250
        setslope := 80
        setslopem := -80
```

```
            pulsedrop := 255
            maxpulse := 245
        TRUE
          SEQ
            tc := 125
            step := 125
            setslope := 160
            setslopem := -160
            pulsedrop := 140
            maxpulse := 120

  -- initial calculation variables
  mem := 19999
  campm := -10000
  campp := 10000
  select := campp
  selectm := campm
  auto := (2*campp)
  autom := (2*campm)
  Vamp := Vampbase
  Vampin := Vampbase
  leap := 0
  Tab1 := 255
  Tab2 := 50
  Tab3 := 50
  tab1last := 20
  tab2last := 20
  tab3last := 20

  -- initial addresses
  count1 := baseadd
  count2 := baseadd + 6667
  count3 := baseadd + 13333
  add1 := baseadd
  add2 := baseadd + 6667
  add3 := baseadd + 333
  toggle1 := 1
  toggle2 := 1
  toggle3 := -1
```

APPENDIX 9.3

Carrierwave Process

```
  WHILE TRUE
    SEQ
      TIME ? now
      interrupt1 ! campm        -- trough of carrierwave
      TIME ? AFTER (now + step)
      TIME ? now
      interrupt1 ! campp   -- peak of carrierwave
      TIME ? AFTER (now + step)     -- wait 1/2 cycle
```

APPENDIX 9.4

PWM Calculation Process

```
WHILE TRUE
  SEQ
    interrupt1 ? carrieramp
    TIME ? y

    -- output pulses
    c[BYTE 0] := Tab1
    c[BYTE 2] := Tab2
    c[BYTE 4] := Tab3
    -- load counter 1
    BYTE.SLICE.OUTPUT(link1,b,12,1)   --address counter
    BYTE.SLICE.OUTPUT(link2,c,0,1)    --count value
    BYTE.SLICE.OUTPUT(link1,b,14,1)   --write count
    ... load counter 2
    ... load counter 3
    -- enable counters
    BYTE.SLICE.OUTPUT(link1,b,17,1)   --enable count

    -- setslope
    IF
      carrieramp > 0
        slope := setslope
      TRUE
        slope := setslopem

    -- increment pointers
    -- pointer 1
    count1 := count1 + leap    -- increment for next si
                               -- value
    IF
      count1 >= (topaddr +9999) -- check if > 360 degree
        count1 := count1 - mem
      TRUE
        SKIP
    IF
      count1 >= (topaddr)   -- check if between 180 and
        SEQ
          add1 := count1 - 10000
          toggle1 := -1
        TRUE
          SEQ
            add1 := count1
            toggle1 := 1
    ... pointer 2
    ... pointer 3
    Vamp := Vampin

    -- calculate pulsewidths
    -- sine table
```

```
GETBYTE(sine1,add1)          -- look up sine
GETBYTE(sine2,add2)          -- look up sine
GETBYTE(sine3,add3)          -- look up sine
-- Tab1
Vmod := (Vamp * sine1)*toggle1
h := carrieramp - Vmod
IF    -- check for automatic pulsedropping
  (h > auto) OR (h < autom)
    SEQ
      Tab1 := pulsedrop
      tab1last := Tab1
  TRUE           -- if not
    SEQ
      Tab1 := h / slope   -- result is in us
      IF    -- check if Vmod > carrieramp
        Tab1 < 0      -- if so
          SEQ
            IF      -- if so check for minpulse or
            -- pulsedrop
              tab1last < pulsedrop
                SEQ
                  IF  -- if pulse too short
                    ((tc - tab1last)) < minpulse

                      SEQ  -- extend
                        Tab1 := minpulse - (tc -
                                      tab1last)
                        tab1last := Tab1
                    TRUE
                      SEQ
                        Tab1 := 3  -- for correct
                                   -- clocking
                        tab1last := Tab1
              TRUE
                SEQ
                  Tab1 := pulsedrop
                  tab1last := Tab1
        TRUE           -- if not
          SEQ
            IF -- check if coming out of pulsedrop
              tab1last < pulsedrop   -- if not
                SEQ
                  IF   -- check for minpulse
                  -- - if not Tab ok
                    ((tc - tab1last) + Tab1)< minpulse
                      SEQ
                        Tab1 := (minpulse - (tc
                                      -tab1last))
                        tab1last := Tab1
                    TRUE
                      tab1last := Tab1
              TRUE                 -- if so
                SEQ
                  IF  -- check if new pulse to be
```

```
                              -- ignored
                   (h1last>auto) OR (h1last<autom)
                      SEQ         -- if so pulsedrop
                         Tab1 := pulsedrop
                         tab1last := minpulse
                   TRUE
                      tab1last := Tab1

   -- check pulse is not too long
   IF
      (Tab1 > maxpulse) AND (Tab1 <> pulsedrop)
         SEQ
            Tab1 := maxpulse
            tab1last := maxpulse
      TRUE
         SKIP

   -- check pulse is not too short
   IF
      (Tab1 < 3)
         SEQ
            Tab1 := 3
            tab1last := 3
      TRUE
         SKIP

   h1last := h

   ... Tab2
   ... Tab3

   -- update the variables
   ALT
      update2 ? leap
         update2 ? Vampin
      TIME ? AFTER (y + 1) -- ignore update if no time
         SKIP
```

APPENDIX 9.5

Update Process (Software Buffer)

```
WHILE TRUE
   SEQ
      update1 ? p
      update1 ? q
      update2 ! p
      update2 ! q
```

APPENDIX 9.6

The Host's Update Routine

```
... declare variables
... declare channels
... declare constants
... declare procedures

SEQ
  fc := 5
  fold := 0
  WHILE (fc <> 2) AND (fc <> 4)
    SEQ
      SendString(Screen,"*n*c enter reqd carrier freq (2 or
                                                       4) ")
      ReadParameters(Keyboard,str)
      FromString(str,fc,ok)
      SendString(Screen,str)
  IF
    fc = 4
      k1 := 1
    TRUE
      k1 := 2

  -- display conditions
  ToString(fc,str)
  SendString(Screen,"*n*c carrier frequency is ")
  SendString(Screen,str)
  SendString(Screen,"kHz")

  -- start pwm
  write.byte.to.link(fc)

  -- update
  Vampl := Vampbase
  WHILE TRUE
    SEQ
      ToString(fold,str)
      SendString(Screen,"*n*n*c running at ")
      SendString(Screen,str)
      SendString(Screen,"*n*n*c input the new frequency")
      SendString(Screen," (0-600 1/10hz)   ")
      ReadParameters(Keyboard,str)
      FromString(str,fnew,ok)
      SendString(Screen,str)
      SendString(Screen,"*n*c is it ok  (y/n) ?
                         -- q stops")
      Keyboard ? frok
      IF(((fnew>=0)AND(fnew<=600))AND
        ((frok='y')OR(frok='Y')))
        SEQ
          SendString(Screen,"*n*c wait")
```

```
fdiff := fnew - fold
IF
  fdiff < 0
    SEQ
      fdiff := (-1)*fdiff
      sign := -1
  TRUE
    sign := 1
freqstep := fdiff

SEQ i = [0 FOR freqstep]
  SEQ
    TIME ? present
    fold := fold + sign  -- .1hz change/50ms
    angle := ((k1 * fold)/4)  --.018 degree
    IF
      fold < minfreq
        Vampl := Vampbase
      TRUE
        Vampl := fold/k
    TIME ? AFTER (present + 780) --50ms
    write.byte.to.link(angle)
    write.byte.to.link(Vampl)

frok = 'q'
  STOP

TRUE
  SEQ
    SendString(Screen,"*n*c input error  -  wait")
    SKIP
```

Chapter 10

The use of transputer parallelism for the GMDH identification algorithm

S.B. Hasnain & Professor D.A. Linkens

10.1 INTRODUCTION

The design of a successful control scheme for any system depends on the ability to predict its response during the given operating conditions. This information can be either extracted from the differential equation describing the dynamics of the system or be extrapolated from its measured input-output response map. A comprehensive mathematical description is generally not available, so the approach based on identification is relied upon.

The classical approach in the design of detection and classification has been to determine explicitly all the relevant characteristics of the process being observed and to use these measurements with a simplifying assumption in the design synthesis. Often, the mathematical structure of the classifier is assumed and its design consists of calculating the best or even the appropriate structure and its coefficients from a representative data base.

The Group Method Of Data Handling (GMDH) is intended for the solution of diverse interpolation problems of engineering cybernetics, such as identification of the static and dynamic characteristics of plants, pattern recognition, prediction of random process and events, optimal control and storage of information etc. This paper presents the GMDH algorithm, possibilities of parallelism and the implementation of GMDH on a single Transputer and on a combination of four Transputers.

10.2 GROUP METHOD OF DATA HANDLING(GMDH)

The deterministic approach to complex plant modelling and control often fails because the dynamics of the sub-components and their inter-connections are not easily understood. The information available is not enough to construct differential equations for the system, so a different approach based on predictive polynomials is tried. The prediction polynomial is a regression equation which connects future values of all input and output variables. Regression analysis allows us to evaluate the coefficients of the polynomial by the criterion of mean square error. The polynomial description of a system determines its ability, performance and invariance, and can be used for the synthesis of an optimal control system.

Polynomial description is determined in two ways:

(a) From a differential equation, by replacing the time derivatives with finite differences.

(b) By performing regression analysis on the sampled input and output observation of the system.

The Group Method Of Data Handling(GMDH) based on the principle of heuristic self organization belongs to the second group. It was first presented by the Russian scientist A.G. Ivakhnenko [1]. Since then, a great deal of attention has been given to this method both inside and outside the U.S.S.R [2]. It is considered to be a powerful method for the identification of non-linear systems because it avoids the increasing computational load to determine the order and parameters in the identified models.

To make these ideas clear, suppose that the input consists of N observables $X_1, X_2, X_3, ...X_n$. Also suppose that the output, Y, may be considered to be the estimate of some property of the input process. In general, Y will be some non-linear function of the X as follows,

$$Y(t) = f(X_1, X_2, ...X_n)$$

(10.1)

The problem is to determine the unknown structure $f(X_1, X_2, ...X_n)$ from the available past data. For a practical and applicational use, the prediction algorithm should have simplicity, need a small amount of computation time, be well suited for real-time operation and applicable to a small amount of available data. Let us assume that $f(X_1, X_2, ..., X_n)$ is represented by a polynomial of a certain order with respect to X_i. The Kolmogorov-Gabor polynomial for the stationary stochastic process provides a conceptual basis for eq.(10.1).

$$Y = a_0 + \sum_{i=1}^{N} a_i * X_i + \sum_{i=1}^{N} \sum_{j=1}^{N} a_{ij} * X_i * X_j$$
$$+ \sum_{i=1}^{N} \sum_{j=1}^{N} \sum_{k=1}^{N} a_{ijk} * X_i * X_j * X_k$$

(10.2)

The Kolmogorov-Gabor polynomial requires a large amount of data and computation of high-dimensional matrices to determine the large number of coefficients of eq.(10.2). The GMDH provides us with an alternative to deal with matrices of large dimension, and makes it possible to solve complex problems when the data sequence is relatively small.

The GMDH can be realized by many algorithms which differ with respect to the construction of the complete description. The most commonly used is the multilayered perception type structure shown in Fig.10.1. It uses partial polynomials of second order and self-sampling thresholds.

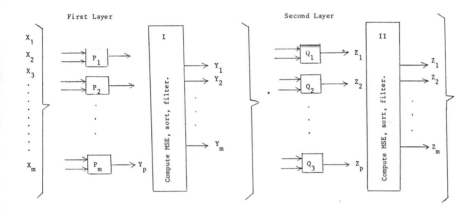

Fig.10.1 GMDH schematic

The basic steps in constructing a GMDH description of a process are as follows:

1. The original data is divided into training and checking sequences, the separation rule being a very heuristic one. Usually the training and the checking sequences are taken alternately or on the basis of the magnitude of the variance from the mean value.

2. Quadratic polynomials are formed for all possible combination of X_i variables taking two at a time, e.g. for 3 variables X_1, X_2, X_3, the following sets of polynomial result:

$$Y_1 = P_1(X_1, X_2) = a_{10} + a_{11}*X_1 + a_{12}*X_2 + a_{13}*X_1*X_1$$
$$+ a_{14}*X_2*X_2 + a_{15}*X_1*X_2$$

$$Y_2 = P_2(X_1, X_3) = a_{20} + a_{21}*X_1 + a_{22}*X_3 + a_{23}*X_1*X_1$$
$$+ a_{24}*X_3*X_3 + a_{25}*X_1*X_3$$

$$Y_3 = P_3(X_2, X_3) = a_{30} + a_{31}*X_2 + a_{32}*X_3 + a_{33}*X_2*X_2$$
$$+ a_{34}*X_3*X_3 + a_{35}*X_2*X_3$$

3. For each polynomial, a system of Normal Gaussian equations is constructed using all the data points in the training set. By solving these equations, the values of the intermediate variables Y_i are determined.

4. The models are used to predict the system response in the training set data region. The predictions are passed through some form of selection criteria, the most widely referred to being the mean square error (MSE).

$$MSE = (1/NC) \cdot \sum_{i=1}^{NC} S \quad \{ Y(t) - Y^n(t) \}^2,$$

where $Y^n(t)$ denotes the predicted value, and NC is the number of data points in the checking set.

5. The models Y_1, Y_2, Y_3, are ordered with respect to the smallest MSE. The models with MSE less then a specified threshold are allowed to pass to the next level of GMDH. The number of functions selected at this level is arbitrary.

6. At the next level the independent variables for the new training and checking set are found by mapping the original training and checking sets through the single layer which has been formed.

7. New polynomials are formed according to step 2, and for each layer, steps 2-6 are repeated. As each new layer is formed, the smallest MSE is stored and plotted as a function of layer number Fig.10.2. The procedure is terminated when the smallest overall MSE is reached at any level. The global minimum is the point of optimum complexity for this choice of network heuristics. The Ivakhnenko Polynomial is formed at this point by choosing the best element in the layer of optimum complexity.

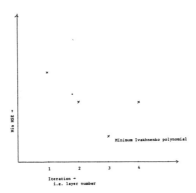

Fig.10.2 Stopping criterion

10.3 SELECTION CRITERIA

Since two different selection methods will rarely select the same group of functions, selection of variables is of prime importance in GMDH. The criteria should be able to take forward the best model in a manner so as not to lose any significant information. The mean square error criterion has a significant weakness since it selects models which sometimes duplicate the information at the expense of discarding useful information. Some other criteria of interest are:

(a)   Regularity criteria
(b)   Minimum bias criteria
(c)   Balance of variable criteria
(d)   Residual criteria

10.4 DEVELOPMENT AND APPLICATIONS OF GMDH

In the early stages, GMDH was applied to the solution of pattern recognition, identification and short range prediction problems. The problems were solved by sifting the models by use of the single external criteria of regularity. Proposals were suggested for dividing the data according to the variation of observation [3]. In 1971, a GMDH algorithm was designed with Bayes formula being used as a reference function [4]. Ivakhnenko and Koppa [5] successfully tried to construct a mathematical model of an ecological system. By predicting the quantity of water in Rybinsk river, it was found that this algorithm can be used not only for qualitative but also for quantitative estimates of any variable of interest. Duffy [6] modified the basic GMDH to implement it on an environmental system. The modification suggests a reduced number of terms in the final model equation and the prediction accuracy seems to improve. This can also be used with systems characterized by many variables and parameters, ill-defined mathematical structures and limited data.

For application in real-time estimation and control, Ikeda presented a sequential GMDH [7]. This algorithm alleviates the problems of real-time computing by employing on-line identification and control. The improved results obtained by Ikeda for a simulated non-linear system, and an application to a non-stationary river flow prediction problem justify the usefulness of this algorithm. Kikot and Patereu [8] used GMDH to construct a mathematical model of the variation of resistivity,R, of metals as a function of temperature,T. Khomovnenko and Kolomiets [9] constructed a model of winter wheat productivity, where partial models were organised using small groups of arguments, rather than constructing one general model. Pokrass and Golubeva [10] presented a mathematical model for long range planning of the cost of coal mining. Karnazes and Bonnel [11] formulated a procedure for using GMDH in the area of system identification. The data vectors which contain the most information concerning the data structure are selected by using information filtering, a procedure which extracts data structure information by clustering the vectors in the input/output database. A non-linear single effect vaporizer with load distribution and set point changes was identified using this GMDH technique. Ivakhnenko and Osipenko [12] suggested that rare events in natural and technological systems can be predicted at the instant of beginning to malfunction from the instant of its last check. However, the prediction is entirely dependent on the number of monitoring measurements of the basic characteristics of the complex device.

10.5 GMDH AND PARALLEL PROCESSING

Different identification methods with specific ranges of applicability have been invented but a common feature of all such methods is the fact that they are realized in the form of sequential computer programs which significantly increases the computer running time. GMDH offers wide possibilities of paralleling of information processing operations in the construction of models of controlled objects [13].

In constructing the multilayer GMDH, all independent variables in one layer are combined, two at a time, to predict the local polynomial. These combinations can be considered as separate independent blocks performing the same task on different inputs. In a hardware realization it is important to isolate blocks , and to organize communication between these blocks in such a way that it is independent of the specific realization of these blocks. The architecture of the transputer facilitates the implementation of these blocks in the construction of a parallel processing system.

The GMDH algorithm could be made more efficient if an array of transputers is used, where each block is calculated by a different transputer, thus significantly reducing the computer running time.

10.6 GMDH ON TRANSPUTER

In order to code the GMDH algorithm in occam, the main algorithm is divided into a number of small processes. Each process is independent in itself and communicate with the other processes over channels. If we have three independent variables in the first layer, three combinations result in estimating three local polynomials as shown in Fig.10.3, which are then processed further by the given selection criteria. In the second layer, another set of local polynomials is determined in a similar manner.

Layer 1: 3 Independent Variables X_1 X_2 + X_3

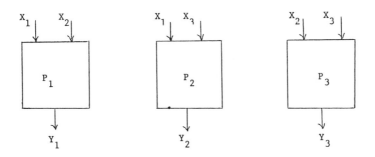

Fig.10.3 Layer 1: Independent variables X_1, X_2 and X_3
- Combinations to estimate the three polynomials

In order to make the algorithm more efficient, an array of three transputers has been used, as shown in Fig.10.4. The process to calculate the Ivakhnenko Polynomial, from the combination of two independent variables, is transmitted from the host to the three slave transputers and each one is provided with a different input. The three transputers perform their work simultaneously and calculate the required polynomials. These calculated values are transmitted back to the host and further calculations regarding the MSE are performed, prior to moving to the next layer of the GMDH algorithm.

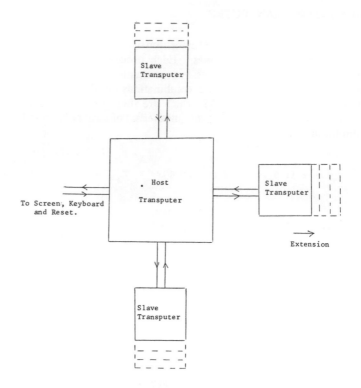

Fig.10.4 Transputer network

The data set from Draper and Smith [14], was used in the sample run. It consists of three independent variables, X_1 - radiation in relative gram calories, X_2 - average soil moisture tension and X_3 - air temperature in deg. The dependent variable is milligrams of vitamins B2 in turnip green. This data was first used to predict the Ivakhnenko Polynomial on one transputer and then on four transputers. It was noted that the time required by four transputers was about one fourth the time required by one transputer. This difference in time increases with an increase in the number of independent variables. The flow diagram of the GMDH algorithm for four transputers is shown in Fig.10.5.

This idea can be extended to any number of Transputers depending upon the independent variables present in the data. For example, four independent variables require six partial polynomials to be predicted and need seven transputers. Similarly, for five independent variables, eleven transputers are required.

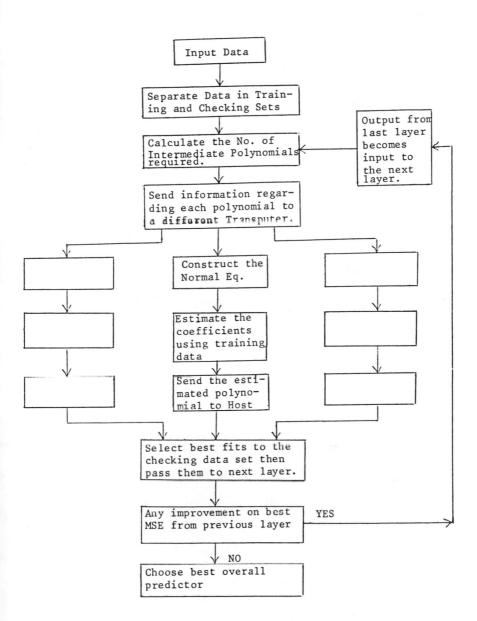

Fig.10.5 Flow diagram of GMDH algorithm on transputers

10.7 GMDH AND MEDICAL DIAGNOSIS

Decision-making in medicine has always been an area of interest for AI researchers. Decision making involves a decision rule applied to a patients measurement vector to decide between possible disease in a differential diagnosis, between possible treatments and between possible prognoses. The significant improvement in time-saving by using the transputer for the GMDH can be used to aid the decision-making process. In medical decision-making, if the number of variables is too large or immediate treatment is to be provided, the mathematical model constructed by GMDH can be used in accordance with some knowledge-based system. The parallelism will provide a faster system which could construct the model on the provided data, and help the tree structure of the knowledge-based system to diagnose the disease accurately. Results of medical data, processed by GMDH, to aid the decision making process are presented.

Numerous investigations in recent years indicate the existence of a cardiac abnormality specific to diabetes mellitus. The autonomic nervous system provides cardiac neurohumoral stimuli which modulate heart-rate and contractility. In addition ,the autonomic nervous system affects loading conditions of the heart through the control of peripheral vascular resistance. Changes in any of these autonomically controlled parameters could contribute to much of the abnormal cardiac function. The data were obtained from a study designed to delineate and compare the cardiac function in long term asymptomatic insulin dependent diabetic patients with and without cardiac autonomic neuropathy (CAN) [15].

Insulin-dependent diabetic patients were enrolled from the endocrine in-patient ward and out-patient clinics. Insulin dependence was determined by history,prior episodes of diabetic ketoacidosis,and the absence of obesity. Ten patients were men and 20 were women, patients ages ranged from 19-53 yr and the duration of diabetes mullitus ranged from 10-28yr. From the results of CAN testing, diabetic complication score and norepinephrine measurements the following three independent variables

(a)   Heart-Rate(bpm)
(b)   Orthostatic Systolic Blood Pressure Drop
(c)   Valsava ratio

and the dependent variable AFS (Autonomic Function Score) were selected. It was observed from the data that the value of AFS greater then 2 showed presence of CAN which was selected as the threshold value to predict CAN in this case. The two significant variables found were (a) and (b) respectively. The Ivakhnenko polynomial and the results of this case along with diagnosis for three patients are shown in Tables 1 and 2.

TABLE 1

Number of Independent Variables = 3
Number of Observations = 17
Number of Variables in Training Set = 12

INPUT DATA

OBS	AFS	HEART RATE	BP DROP	VALSALVA RATIO
TRAINING SET				
1	2.00	92.0	4.0	1.00
2	0.01	42.0	4.0	1.16
3	3.00	96.0	36.0	1.06
4	4.00	122.0	28.0	1.04
5	2.00	96.0	32.0	1.13
6	0.02	90.0	10.0	1.16
7	0.02	83.0	20.0	1.55
8	2.00	86.0	8.0	1.06
9	4.00	90.0	65.0	1.03
10	2.00	96.0	36.0	1.36
11	4.00	88.0	40.0	1.00
12	0.02	84.0	10.0	1.66
CHECKING SET				
13	0.03	73.0	2.0	1.11
14	2.00	76.0	30.0	1.10
15	0.02	90.0	12.0	2.12
16	1.00	90.0	14.0	1.18
17	5.00	112.0	32.0	1.00

Level Number = 1
Number of Variables Saved = 3
RMIN Value Over Checking Set = 0.2219E + 00

AFS = Automatic Function Score
Heart Rate = Heart Beat Per Minute
B.P. Drop = Orthostatic Systolic Blood Pressure Drop.

IVAKHNENKO POLYNOMIAL
(Printed Only if G.M.D.H. Converged in One Layer)

$$Y = A + B*U + C*V + D*U*U + +E*V*V + F*U*V$$

A = 0.44748E + 01	D = 0.18855E-02	U = X(1) Heart rate
B = -0.21001E + 00	E = 0.42251E-03	V = X(2) B.P. drop
C = 0.41519E + 00	F = -0.43094E-02	

TABLE 2

CASE NO.1

Give the value for variable X1 (Heart Rate)
90.00
Give the value for variable X3(B.P. Drop)
14.00
Autonomic function is less than 2.00 C.A.N. not predicted

CASE NO.2

Give the value for variable X1 (Heart Rate)
130.00
Give the value for variable X3 (B.P. Drop)
4.00
Autonomic function is greater than 2.00 C.A.N. predicted.

The second data concerns the Growth Hormone and Glucose in diabetic patients [16]. It is extracted from a study conducted to examine the changes in plasma levels of Human Growth Hormone(HGH) in severe diabetics under conditions resembling Hypoglycemic reaction. Hypoglycemia is a recognised stimulus for augmenting plasma human growth levels. HGH behaviour in severe diabetics with high levels of Blood Glucose (BG) and normal subjects were observed before, during and after Hypoglycemia induced by insulin.

The tests were performed in a metabolic ward. With the diabetic patients, prolonged regulation of the diabetes with diet and insulin preceded each test. Normal subjects followed a similar dietary regimen but had no therapy with insulin. The data consist of tests on normal and diabetic subjects whose HGH increased only or mainly during Hypoglycemia. The three independent variables are

(a) Insulation Infusion,
(b) Plasma Human Growth Hormone(ng/ml) base-line and
(c) Plasma Human Growth Hormone(ng/ml) during Hypoglycemia(peak).

Blood Glucose level mg/100 ml was selected as the dependent variable, Since the original data consist of observations on both normal and diabetic patients, a diabetic patient can be detected if the predicted value of the Blood Glucose is higher then the threshold level, i.e. 200 mg/ml in this case. The two significant variables found by GMDH, i.e. (b) and (c) and the Ivakhnenko Polynomial were used to predict the value of Blood Glucose. The original data, the Ivakhnenko polynomial and the diagnoses of three patients are shown in Tables 3 and 4 respectively.

TABLE 3

Number of Independent Variables = 3
Number of Observations = 12
Number of Variables in Training Set = 8

INPUT DATA

OBS	B.G(BASE)	INSF	PL.HIGH	PL.HGH HYP
TRAINING SET				
1	350.00	19.00	5.6	40.00
2	309.00	16.20	3.4	72.50
3	67.00	5.90	3.7	23.50
4	382.00	53.70	6.0	100.01
5	83.00	8.20	1.7	72.50
6	399.00	17.20	3.9	25.00
7	398.00	20.70	2.8	19.00
8	84.00	7.70	0.9	60.00
CHECKING SET				
9	78.00	8.50	2.6	56.00
10	305.00	42.90	2.88	5.00
11	84.00	5.50	1.9	10.00
12	72.00	8.20	4.16	9.00

Level Number = 1
Number of Variables Saved = 3
RMIN Value Over Checking Set = 0.3323E + 00

B.G.(Base)	=	Blood Glucose Level (Base Line) ng/100ml.
INSF	=	Insulation Infusion (Units)
PL Hgh	=	Plasma Human Growth Hormone (BASE) ng/ml.
PL Hgh Hyp	=	Plasma Human Growth Hormone During Hypoglycemia ng/ml.

IVAKHNENKO POLYNOMIAL
(Printed Only if G.M.D.H. Converged in One Layer)

$$Y = A + B*U + C*V + D*U*U + E*V*V + F*U*V$$

A = -0.42524E + 02
B = -0.69926E + 00   U = X(1)   Insulin Fusion
C = 0.802297E + 00   V = X(2)   Plasma H.G.H.
D = -0.11731E-02
E = -0.30406E-02
F = 0.32311E-02

TABLE 4

CASE NO.1

Give the value for variable X1 (Insulin Infusion)
17.20
Give the value for variable X3(Plasma H.G.H.)
2.80
Blood Glucose Level is Higher Diabetes Predicted

CASE NO.2

Give the value for variable X1 (Insulin Infusion)
5.60
Give the value for variable X3 (Plasma H.G.H.)
4.30
Blood Glucose Level is Lower Diabetes Not Predicted

REFERENCES

1. Ivakhnenko,A.G., 1968, : "The group method of data handling - a rival of stochastic approximation", Soviet automatic Control, Vol.13, No.3.

2. Farlow,S.J., 1980, "Self Organizing methods in modeling GMDH type algorithms", Marcel Dekker Inc.

3. Ivakhnenko,A.G, 1971, "Polynomial theory of complex numbers", IEEE Trans. Sys. Man Cyb., Vol.SMC-1.

4. Ivakhnenko,A.G. and Koppa.Yu.V., 1970, "Regularization of Decision Function in the Group Method Of Data Handling", Soviet Automatic Control, Vol. 3.

5. Ivakhnenko,A.G. and Koppa.Yu.V, 1971, "Mathematical Simulation Of Complex Ecological Systems", Soviet Automatic Control, Vol. 4.

6. Duffy,J.J., 1975, "A learning identification algorithm and its application to an environmental system", IEEE Sys. Man Cyb., Vol.SMC-5.

7. Ikeda Subaro, Mikiko Ochiai, 1976, "Sequential GMDH algorithm and its application to river flow prediction, IEEE Trans Sys. Man Cyb., Vol.SMC-6.

8. Kokot,V.S., Patareu,S.G., 1980, "Processing of experimentally measured densities of Metals Using GMDH", Soviet Automatic Control, Vol.13.

9. Khomovnenko,M.G. and Kolomiets, N.G., 1980, "Self organization of a system of single partial models for predicting the wheat harvest", Soviet Automatic Control, Vol.13.

10. Pokrass,V.L. and Golubeva,L.V, 1980, "Self organization of a mathematical model for long range planning of the cost of coal mining", Soviet Automatic Control, Vol.13.

11. Karnazes,P.A. and Bonnel,R.D, 1982, "System identification techniques using Group Method Of Data Handling", IFAC, 1982, U.S.A.

12. Ivakhnenko,A.G. and Osipenko,V.V, 1980, "Prediction of rare events on the basis of GMDH algorithm", Soviet Automatic Control, Vol.13.

13. Belozerskiy,Y.E., Ivakhnenko,A.G. and Kozuborskiy,S.F., 1980, "Synthesis of control model using multilayer GMDH algorithm", Soviet Automatic Control, Vol.14, No.1.

14. Draper,N.R. and Smith,H., 1966, "Applied regression analysis", Wiley, New York.

15. Zola,B., Kahn,J.K., Juni,J.E. and Vinik,A.I., 1986, "Abnormal Cardiac function in diabetic patients with autonomic neuropathy in the absence of ischemic heart disease", Journal Of Clinical Endocrinology and Metabolism, Vol.63, No.1.

16. Fatourechi,V., Molner,G.D., Ackerman,E., Rosevear,J.W., Moxness,K.E. and Taylor,W.F., 1969, "Growth hormone and glucose interrelationships in Diabetes : Studies with insulation infusion during continuous blood glucose analysis", Journal Of Clinical Endocrinology and Metabolism, Vol.29, Pt.1.

Alternative architectures

Following the exclusive consideration of the Transputer in the preceding Section, three alternative architectures are considered here. The evolution of a parallel processing computer for flight control is described. Careful consideration of communication requirements for this application resulted in the specification of a network communication strategy which does not exhibit system expansion difficulties. It is instructive to follow the historical development of this asynchronous multiprocessor system.

Turning from a medium-grain to a fine-grain approach to parallel processing, the Occam programming language is used to simulate a parallel Kalman filter in an exploration of the potential of a systolic array architecture. Hitherto, the computational burden arising from its associated matrix operations has limited the applicability of this important estimation tool. Through decomposition of the algorithm to a set of basic calculations, an important algorithmic approach emerges which is accessible to parallel processing.

Finally, the PACE (Programmable Adaptive Computing Engine) chip is introduced. This is a fine-grain programmable component based on the cellular automata approach, with cells capable of performing a variety of primitive control functions. A fascinating programming prospect which arises out of this development is the opportunity of mapping graphical representations of controllers directly onto the cellular array.

Chapter 11

The evolution of a parallel processing computer for flight control

D.P.M. Wills

11.1 SUMMARY

Over the past few years, studies have been conducted at British Aerospace, Brough into the application of asynchronous parallel processing in flight control. Initial multiprocessor designs were aimed at research activities in digital control, but it was soon appreciated that they also offered several advantages for production aircraft. Outlined within this Chapter is the history of the development of the flight control system together with some of its applications.

11.2 INTRODUCTION

Modern military aircraft are required to perform in an ever increasing performance envelope, providing acceptable response characteristics for a wide range of flight conditions. This aim for greater aerodynamic performance has led to aircraft designs that no longer have a natural stability, impossible to control by the unaided pilot and hence the introduction of a flight computer has become essential for the implementation of complex feedback control systems to restore suitable handling properties. This process of design has now reached such a stage that some current (F16, F18, Experimental Aircraft Project - E.A.P.) and many future combat aircraft (European Fighter Aircraft - E.F.A.) are totally reliant on the correct operation of the Flight Control System (F.C.S.). In order to achieve the high integrity required by the F.C.S., in the order of only one total failure in 10^7 flying hours, a triplex or quadruplex system is usually implemented.

Initial implementations of such flight control systems (i.e. for the F16) have been designed using analogue electronics, leading to a restriction on the type and complexity of the control laws used. These problems have led designers towards a fully digital computer for the F.C.S., allowing far greater flexibility for control law design and implementation together with the ability to include extensive built-in-test (B.I.T.) and pre-flight- test (P.F.T.). However, the overall architecture has remained much the same as many identical computing lanes are employed to give overall reliability and integrity to the system.

Using digital computing, therefore, has many advantages in its flexibility and reduction in hardware size and cost, however it soon becomes apparent that the associated software overheads become more dominant in the overall system cost. The flight critical nature of the F.C.S. demands that extensive tests must be conducted on the coded software before it is allowed to be flown and, that during flight, considerable cross-checking is required between lanes to guard against computer failure. Since most commercial flight control systems are based upon a single processor (bit-slice) solution there is also a large software overhead associated with scheduling the operation of each segment of control law/management task.

Once all the management tasks are included within the total software budget, the control laws reduce to less than 30% of the task, and, in order to gain a fast iteration cycle, much of the code is written in assembler. This again results in higher costs but also extends timescales and increases the problem of software verification.

In the late 1970's and early 1980's B.Ae. Brough wished to perform various control law designs on a flight vehicle (R.A.E. Farnborough's A.C.T. Hunter). It was recognised that the then current digital systems might be acceptable for production aircraft but they were too expensive and lacked the flexibility needed for research. Hence began the development of a flight control system based upon parallel processing using simple microprocessing elements.

11.3 AN EARLY EXPERIMENTAL MULTI-PROCESSOR SYSTEM

11.3.1 Proposed Architecture

With an aim to reduce software overheads an attempt was made to partition software into a number of well-defined modules that could only interact in a limited (and specified) way, which should aid in the specification, implementation, modification and verification. This type of partitioning has been implemented on ground-based systems using specialised operating systems (MASCOT) and has the considerable advantage that, since the interface between modules is well defined, an individual module may be removed, modified, re-validated and then replaced without the need of re-testing the complete system. However the technique needs the overhead of a complex operating system which would negate its advantages when implemented for flight control. Therefore, to retain the advantages of software partitioning with the need of a complex executive, the hardware was also partitioned - i.e. each software module implemented upon its own micro- processor with I/O allocated to individual hardware links. Such an approach also leads to a considerable increase in program iteration since many of its components run in parallel, and this increase in speed may be used to further simplify the software overhead with the introduction over a medium-level control language.

Essential to any parallel processing architecture is the communication strategy: an incorrect choice can totally negate all advantages gained from the increase in processing power. If a bus structure is chosen then its throughput can constrain the system expansion and introduce variable time delays dependent upon its loading. If dual-port memory is used then it limits the number of processors that may be attached. More advanced techniques such as packet switching could alleviate these problems but their complexity ruled them out of a low cost, quick solution. With these difficulties in mind, and the knowledge that the early control laws being investigated had minimal communication between software modules (although the overall communication could be quite high), a network communication strategy was adopted.

A communication strategy based upon a network does not exhibit system expansion difficulties since the inclusion of new processor elements also increases the communication bandwidth. If the links between processors are constrained to carry only control data rather than information inherently required for F.C.S. operation, then many software/hardware faults within a module may be localised, allowing the feasibility of some fault recovery.

The data being transmitted between processing modules in a real-time control application consist of a number of variables each representing a continuous function of time. In this early architecture, each variable was allocated a unique communication channel (which happened to be analogue) allowing for convenient monitoring and the disposal of any handshake routines, since a variable can only be overwritten by itself. Since a single variable is often required by more than one processor, a single source/multi-sink network was implemented using A/D and D/A converters for an analogue realisation.

11.3.2 Processor Implementation

Having decided to investigate a multi-processor system, where all processors run asynchronously in order to minimise the software overhead required for synchronisation, (hence later the computing architecture was named A.M.P.S. - Asynchronous Multi-Processor System), the first task was choose a microprocessor that was commercially available and could demonstrate the above- mentioned features. The relatively large number of processor elements required in the system indicated the use of a single-chip microcomputer in order to keep the volume of the final system practical. The simple technique adopted for the asynchronous communication was analog and hence it was also desirable that the chosen microcomputer had A/D and D/A converters. Finally, it was expected that repeated reprogramming would be required and therefore on-board EPROM was essential. The sum of these conditions left only one device, the Intel 2920 Analog Signal Processor (see Fig. 11.1).

- Real Time Digital Processing of Analog Signals

- Nominal Signal Bandwidths from DC to 10KHz

- Digital Processing Accuracy and Stability

- Special Purpose Instruction Set for Signal Processing

- Twenty five Bit Wide Data Word

- 400 ns Instruction Execution Time

- Multiple Analog Inputs (4) and Outputs (8)

- On-Chip Sample and Hold Circuits and D/A Converter

- On-Chip EPROM: User Programmable and UV Erasable

- On-Chip Scratch Pad Memory (40 Locations)

- Analog and/or TTL Output Waveforms, User Selectable

- 192 Program Locations

(a)

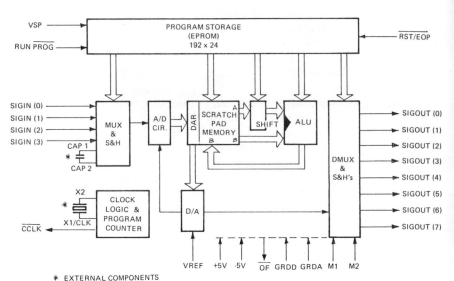

(b)

**Fig.11.1 INTEL 2920: (a) Summary of processor features
(b) Functional block diagram of architecture.**

However, the 2920 has some undesirable properties which, although not effecting the proving of various concepts, would prejudice its use as the main processor in real applications. The main limitations are:-

(a) I/O resolution of only 9 bits
(b) Limited Instruction Set (later seen to be desirable)
(c) Limited program space
(d) A new device of uncertain pedigree.

For demonstration of the system, various software techniques were used to overcome these shortfalls (at the expense also of some external hardware) and a multi-processor board was developed (see Fig.11.2).

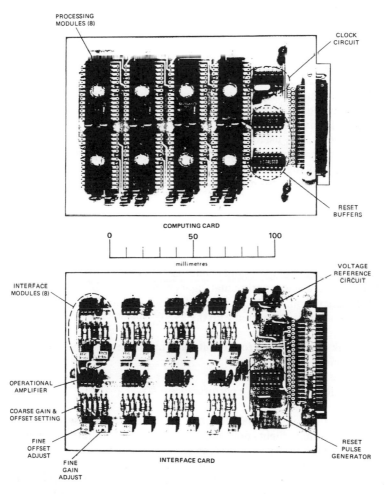

Fig.11.2 Example computing and interface cards

The lack of a branch instruction in the 2920 was initially seen as a problem but later it was realised that removing branching from a control program helped to alleviate a number of context dependent failures. It can also be of aid to the actual control software construction since every instruction is executed once and hence the software cycle time is constant (useful for integrators, etc.). However the main draw-back is the increase in computation time (alleviated somewhat by the increase in processing capability supplied by the multi-processing environment).

11.3.3 Interface Module

It was essential that this system could be used with existing analog equipment and, although the 2920 has A/D and D/A converters, additional buffering, anti-aliasing filter and gain control are required. These requirements were implemented on a separate interface card and connection was made to the processors again via the analogue links.

Hence a system was able to be constructed from these two basic modules that allowed early experimentation into digitally implemented control laws using a multi-processor system. Various test procedures were carried out in a laboratory environment and boxes were soon produced for successful flight within the R.A.E.'s Experimental Tornado Drop Model. The next stage of testing was in the R.A.E. Hunter. However little useful data was collected from this since, regrettably, the aircraft suffered a catastrophic engine failure on its first flight with the experimental kit aboard - work on flight control at Brough was substantially delayed but sufficient data had been gathered from ground tests to justify further work on a parallel processing F.C.S.

11.4 AMPS 1 - AN F.C.S. WITH GO-FASTER STRIPES

Having identified operational benefits - not only research - for AMPS, work began in designing a new experimental flight control system based upon the previous experience gained from the 2920 design. Various shortfalls of the previous design were addressed largely associated with the 2920:

(a) Lack of suitable I/O (only 9-bits) and insufficient number of analogue links
(b) Limited program space
(c) Slow processing speed
(d) Difficulties in reliable performance.

Although this system was designed for experimental use it was also to be required for many more flight applications and hence greater flexibility and reliability was required. At this time it was also seen to be desirable to encourage collaboration with an external avionics contractor in order that the concepts of parallel processing might become more widespread and help reduce overall costs involved in F.C.S. implementation. The result of these efforts in collaboration has been a long term joint venture between British Aerospace, Brough and Lucas Aerospace in the development of AMPS

11.4.1 General Computing Module (G.C.M.)

An AMPS 1 system was constructed mainly from identical computing modules (except for aircraft specific boards such as that required for communication to a 1553 B databus), differing only from the original concepts in that two processors and all I/O is included on each board. A detailed description is now included.

The G.C.M. consists of a Z8002 microprocessor running a 6MHz clock, with 8K words of external programmable EPROM, 2K words of external scratchpad memory, and fully memory- mapped I/O. Each module also includes an Intel 2920 which allows for the inclusion of a dissimilar signal path to aid in monitoring.

The main I/O resources included on each card are as follows.

(a) A 16 channel data acquisition system comprising a 12- bit ADC and 16-channel multiplexer capable of accepting input voltages in the range of +/- 10 V.

(b) Four 12-bit DAC channels, of which one is multiplexed between four sample and holds. In effect this gives rise to a total of 7 outputs.

(c) A disconnect relay.

(d) 8 discrete input channels, all TTL compatible.

(e) 3 discrete output channels, all TTL compatible.

A functional block diagram of a GCM is given in Fig.11.3 and Fig.11.4 is a typical component layout for a card.

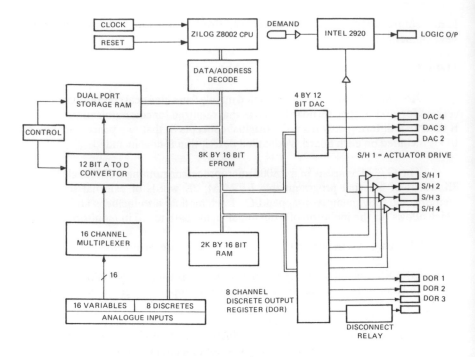

Fig.11.3 Block diagram of AMPS 1 General Computing Module

Fig.11.4 An AMPS 1 General Computing Module

Many AMPS cards have been manufactured by Lucas Aerospace some with slightly different specifications, but all basically conforming to the above standard. Each board, for flight application or bench, has been constructed in a standard format.

Once again, a full parallel processing system has been constructed from a number of individual cards and a typical unit, housed in a 3/4 A.T.R. standard format housing, is illustrated in Fig.11.5.

The backplane allows all I/O inter-connection between external sensors/ actuators and modules. Connection to the backplane from a module is via 96-way connector. Inter-card communication is achieved by dedicated point- to-point hard wiring of input and output pins across the backplane, the input and output channels being connected to a modules 96-way connector via wire-wrap patching which allows each module to be configured as required.

Fig.11.5 A typical AMPS unit

11.4.2 Software

Software is written for the AMPS 1 system using two languages (a far from ideal situation). All code for the main control law processor (Z8002) is written in LUCOL, a high-integrity control language developed by Lucas Aerospace. Each processor in the system has code specifically generated for its execution - no parallel processing facilities are provided in the language and hence separate programs are required. However, various facilities have been developed by Lucas to aid in overall software design and these greatly reduce the problems related to inter-processor communication.

The Intel 2920 is still programmed in its reduced instruction set and its role has now been mainly reduced to watchdog functions.

11.4.3 AMPS 1 Applications

AMPS 1 computing modules have been in several projects and these have led to its application to flight. Various applications have been demonstrated, e.g.

(a) Single and multiple G.C.M. demonstrations
(b) Duo-duplex operation for flight control in the Advanced Systems Demonstrator Rig (A.S.D.R.) based at B.Ae. Brough.
(c) Control of the R.A.E. High Incidence Research Model (H.I.R.M.)
(d) An experimental pitch axis autopilot for the R.A.E./D.T.I. B.A.C. 1-11 at Bedford.

These applications, together with extensive ground testing, have demonstrated the great advantages that may be realised from parallel processing in flight control. The next stage, therefore, in AMPS development is to design a fully digital representative computer system capable of controlling the demanding aerodynamic features being incorporated into modern fighter aircraft.

11.5 AMPS 2 (A FULLY DIGITAL SYSTEM) AND BEYOND

The concept of AMPS has been well proven using the AMPS 1 system but a number of limitations may be highlighted in view of actual F.C.S. applications. These lie in two main areas:

(a) Supplying I/O on every module implies a large overhead of unused hardware and therefore increased size.

(b) The analogue communications suffer from a lack of bandwidth, speed and accuracy.

In light of these two areas, together with the ever increasing requirement for speed, a further development was identified - AMPS 2.

11.5.1 Initial System Description

The AMPS 2 flight control system comprises of a number of processor modules, two I/O modules (termed the 'front-end-unit' and 'back-end-unit') and a communication links. Typically, a module will have one transmit line (TX) and four receive lines (RX). Each TX outputs data at up to 20 Mbits/sec in a serial format with a protocol nicknamed H.I.C.U.P. (High Integrity Communications Universal Protocol). Associated with a TX is 256 words of memory and the TX is hardwired to transmit a frame of 2^n words per cycle ($1 \leqslant n \leqslant 8$). Having completed the transmission of a single frame, it starts again. Any RX that is connected to this TX will read in the complete frame and store the contents in its own local memory. The memory area associated with a RX or TX is dual-ported and may be accessed by the main processor on the board. In essence, this mixture of transmitters, receivers and dual-port memory allows a flexible, distributed shared memory system to be implemented.

A processing module comprises of a high speed processor, ROM, RAM, watchdog timers and a number of communication lines (typically four RX and one TX) together with their associated dual-port memory. All data associated with this module arrives via the serial communications (see Fig.11.6). External I/O for sensors, actuators and other lanes is dealt with by the front-end-unit.

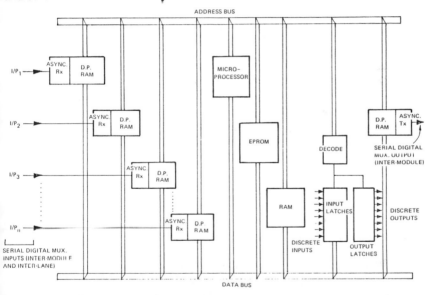

Fig.11.6 Block diagram of AMPS 2 General Computing Module

The front-end-unit is a communications node for all sensor information coming into the lane. All the incoming data associated with the lane is interfaced on this card and combined into a single serial data stream, which is then sent to all other lanes and is also available to all modules in its own computing section.

The back-end-unit provides a means of interfacing the control laws to the actuators, receiving demands from the processor modules and transforming these into suitable analog signals.

A complete system diagram is shown in Fig.11.7.

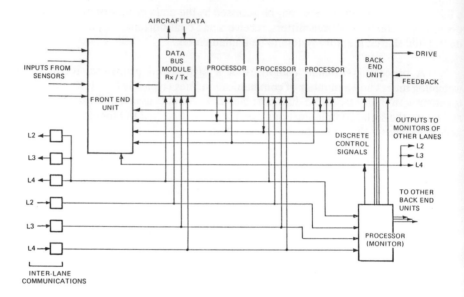

Fig.11.7 AMPS 2 partitioning of Flight Control Unit

11.5.2 Future Implementation

Future designs will likely alter under the influence of new custom design techniques and the communications strategy will be a VLSI implementation. RISC-type processor designs are also under serious consideration. AMPS 2 will likely be at least an order of magnitude faster than any other F.C.S. available now.

11.6 FINAL COMMENTS

The studies in AMPS that have occurred over the last few years at B.Ae. Brough have helped introduce the concept of parallel processing (specifically asynchronous processing) into the world of flight control. Although many problems, both technical and commercial, were encountered in the early years it has been shown that great benefits occur when multiple processor solutions are sought. Also, throughout this period of hardware design and demonstration, new design strategies have been developed for easing the control designers task - in particular a new language is being developed specifically aimed at analog control design for implementation on digital processors, namely the Control Instruction Set (C.I.S.). The combination of both software and hardware points to a future control system that is not only easier to program, modify and validate but also cheaper to build.

As to the future when compared with new parallel processor development, AMPS was generated as a concept which would be adapted to suit the emerging technology, and studies are being carried out to identify the best way ahead.

This work has been carried out with the support of the Procurement Executive, Ministry of Defence.

BIBLIOGRAPHY

Wright S.M. and Winter J.S., A modular approach to high reliability software generation with application to non-linear control, AGARD Conference Proceedings No. 321, Advances in Guidance and Control Systems.

Wright S.M. and Brown J.G., The development of asynchronous multi-processor concepts for flight control system applications, AGARD Conference Proceedings No. 33, Tactical Airborne Distributed Computing and Networks.

Chapter 12

Occam simulation of a systolic architecture for parallel Kalman filtering

Dr. G.W. Irwin & F.M.F. Gaston

12.1 INTRODUCTION

The Kalman filter is a recursive estimator of the states of a dynamic system and is optimal in the sense that the mean square estimation error is minimised. The filter operates in a predict-correct fashion; an internal model of the plant is used for time updates and a feedback scheme provides the measurement updates. It facilitates the practical implementation of state feedback controllers by generating the required estimates of the state vector from noisy measurement data. The Kalman filter may also be used for least squares parameter estimation in plant identification, and as such also finds application in adaptive feedback control where tracking of critical plant parameters is needed. Thus in aerospace applications for example, Kalman filtering techniques are successfully and widely practiced in flight control, tracking and navigation functions.

The applicability of the Kalman filter to broadband real-time processing problems is generally limited, however, by the relative complexity of the matrix computations involved since the number of arithmetic operations required for implementing the algorithm with n state variables is $0(n^2)$ and $0(n^3)$ for the covariance updates.

Parallel processing is making a major impact in digital signal and information processing applications. These require high-speed, real-time computations which must be performed on continuous data streams. The computations involved are highly structured with regular matrix-type operations, a feature shared by Kalman filter algorithms. This has stimulated research into novel architectures for parallel Kalman filtering.

Broadly, there are two design methodologies. The coarse-grained approach exploits natural parallelism at a system level and divides the calculations on this basis. Thus it has been suggested, for example, that the filtering and prediction calculations may be performed on separate processors by forcing the measurement updates to lag the time updates by one sample timestep. This technique is commonly used in applications of transputer hardware and, although practical, suffers in two important respects; first, lack of generality since the resultant parallel implementation is often application dependent and second, the required processing bandwidth may not be achieved. The fine-grained approach on the other hand, attempts to decompose the algorithm into a set of basic calculations through a fundamental reorganisation of the computing architecture, of which systolic arrays are an example. The adoption of the fine-grained technique is an algorithmic design decision and, unlike the coarse-grained one, leaves open the decision as to hardware implementation of the systolic array architecture produced. The choice of custom chip or arrays of transputers may then be made on the basis of factors such as size, cost and computational bandwidth required. Further, it can be argued that such a fundamental examination of the mapping of the Kalman filter and indeed other control algorithms onto parallel architectures is essential if general design strategies and guidelines for parallel processing in real-time control are to emerge.

The aim of the work reported in this paper was to investigate a systolic array architecture for parallel Kalman filtering proposed by Yeh [1], using Occam to simulate the hardware operation. Section 12.2 provides an introduction to systolic arrays for parallel processing and their use in matrix-type calculations. This is followed by a description of the parallel algorithm and associated systolic array, in Sections 12.3 and 12.4 respectively. Occam simulation of the processor array is presented next. Section 12.6 studies the parallel Kalman filter architecture in terms of computational speedup and efficiency of processor usage. Extensions such as scheduling of passes and the use of an array for each pass are analysed.

12.2 SYSTOLIC ARRAYS

As mentioned in the Introduction, parallel processing is making a major impact in digital signal and information processing applications requiring low cost, high-speed computing power. Systolic array networks, in particular, are receiving much attention for dedicated VLSI processors. These are arrays of individual processing cells, each of which has some local memory and is connected only to its nearest neighbours in the form of a regular lattice (Fig.12.1). Each cell can carry out simple logic and a few basic arithmetic operations up to the complexity of square-root calculations. The systolic array architecture is attractive for VLSI technology; multi-processor systems dedicated to real-time matrix computation can be constructed from highly repeated sub-units which simplifies the design and lowers costs. In addition, the communication bottlenecks associated with a conventional single processor architecture are avoided by the distribution of memory and computation across the array and by having only nearest neighbour communication between processors. Data is shunted across the array in a specific direction. On each clock cycle, a cell receives data from its neighbours, performs a specific processing operation on it and stores the resulting data within the cell. This data is then passed to neighbouring cells on the next clock cycle. The concept of a systolic array was first introduced by Kung and Leiserson [2], who used arrays of simple inner product step processors to perform matrix computations, notably LU decomposition. Most important of all, they showed how a hex-connected systolic array could solve systems of linear equations, a computational requirement in many high speed signal processing applications. The subject has expanded rapidly since this early work and a large number of systolic array designs have been proposed for other matrix operations such as orthogonal triangularisation, tridiagonalisation, the computation of eigenvalues and singular value decomposition.

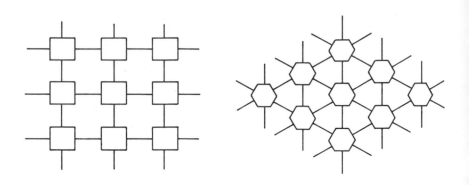

Fig. 12.1 Systolic array meshes

A number of systems have now been built which in current technology take the form of multi-chip circuits constructed on one or more printed circuit boards. The systolic array approach has also been used for the design of individual VLSI chips which work with individual data lists rather than complete data words. For further information on hardware developments in the United Kingdom, see Reference 3.

Figure 12.2 illustrates the inputs and outputs of a single processor. During each clock cycle the processor passes the data on a_i to a_o, passes the data on b_i to b_o and finally computes an inner step product by adding the product of the data on a_i and b_i to that on c_i and passing this sum to c_o. All outputs are latched so that when one processor is connected to another the changing output of one during a clock period will not interfere with the input to another.

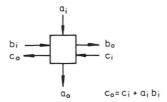

Fig.12.2 Inner product step processor

An array of these processors, connected as shown in Fig.12.3, will perform the matrix times vector computation y $-$ Ax when the order $n = 4$. The elements of y are initialised at zero and pumped from right to left across the array, accumulating the required partial products as they go. Clearly, correct timing of data is crucial for correct operation. Thus for example y_1, x_1 and a_{11} should all arrive at the centre processor at the same time requiring that x_1 and y_1 enter the array at the same time while a_{11} is fed in three timesteps later.

In general, the arrays of processors are more complicated than this. Often, matrix-based parallel algorithms require the interconnection of several different systolic arrays with matrices coming out of one array transposed, triangularised or perhaps upside-down before being passed into the next array. In such cases, it is difficult to visualise precisely what is happening and when, and simulation of the parallel architecture allows checking of the operation of an individual array as well as ensuring that data transfer between different arrays is correct. Simulation studies also provide a convenient means of evaluating the likely hardware performance of different architectures for parallel Kalman filtering.

12.3 PARALLEL ALGORITHM

A computational framework for a parallel Kalman filter, based upon the Fadeev algorithm [4] has been proposed by Yeh. This Section will introduce the Fadeev algorithm and its application to Kalman filtering.

Consider the linear, discrete-time system described by

$$x(k+1) \quad = F(k)x(k) + w(k)$$

$$z(k) \quad = H(k)x(k) + v(k)$$

where $\mathbf{x}(k)$ is the (nx1) state vector and $\mathbf{z}(k)$ is the (mx1) measurement vector. The state transition matrix $F(k)$ and measurement matrix $H(k)$ are of appropriate dimensions. The system and measurement noise sequences $\mathbf{w}(k)$ and $\mathbf{v}(k)$ are assumed to be independent, zero mean and Gaussian with covariance matrices $Q(k)$ and $R(k)$ respectively.

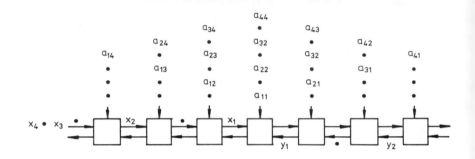

Fig 12.3 Systolic array for the matrix by vector multiplication, $\mathbf{y} = \mathbf{Ax}$

The Kalman filter algorithm for optimal state estimation takes the following form.

Time updates:

$$\hat{\mathbf{x}}(k/k\text{-}1) = F(k\text{-}1)\,\hat{\mathbf{x}}(k\text{-}1/k\text{-}1) \tag{12.1}$$

$$P(k/k\text{-}1) = F(k\text{-}1)\,P(k\text{-}1/k\text{-}1)\,F^T(k\text{-}1) + Q(k\text{-}1) \tag{12.2}$$

Measurement updates:

$$P^{-1}(k/k) = P^{-1}(k/k\text{-}1) + H^T(k)\,R^{-1}(k)\,H(k) \tag{12.3}$$

$$K(k) = P(k/k)\,H^T(k)\,R^{-1}(k) \tag{12.4}$$

$\tilde{z}(k) = z(k) - H(k) x(k/k-1)$ (12.5)

$\hat{x}(k/k) = x(k/k-1) + K(k)\tilde{z}(k)$ (12.6)

The initial conditions are

$\hat{x}(0) = 0$, $P(0/0) = P_0$ or $P^{-1}(0/0) = P_0^{-1}$

The Fadeev algorithm can be introduced in terms of calculating

WB + D (12.7)

given

WA = C, (12.8)

where A, B, C, D are known matrices and W is unknown. Clearly equation (12.8) gives W as

$W = CA^{-1}$

which can be substituted in (12.7) to produce the required result

$CA^{-1}B + D$

The same answer can be arrived at, without the necessity of finding W explicitly, as follows. The matrices A, B, C and D are loaded into the compound matrix of equation (12.9),

$$\begin{bmatrix} A & \vdots & B \\ \hline -C & \vdots & D \end{bmatrix}$$ (12.9)

and a linear combination of the first row is then added to the second to produce

$$\begin{bmatrix} A & \vdots & B \\ \hline -C+WA & \vdots & D+WB \end{bmatrix}$$ (12.10)

If W, which specifies the linear combination, is chosen such that

-C + WA = 0 (12.11)

then the matrix in equation (12.10) becomes

$$\begin{bmatrix} A & B \\ 0 & D+CA^{-1}B \end{bmatrix} \qquad (12.12)$$

and the lower right quadrant now contains the answer. The Fadeev algorithm then involves reducing C to zero, in the compound matrix of equation (12.9), by ordinary row manipulation of the Gaussian elimination type. The required matrix calculation is produced in the bottom right quadrant.

A range of matrix computations can be performed by proper choice of A, B, C and D. Thus for example if

$$B=I, C=I, D=0$$

then A^{-1} will be generated. In particular Yeh showed that the matrix equations (12.1)-(12.6) of the Kalman filter algorithm could be produced in eight successive passes of the Fadeev algorithm as shown in Table 12.1. The matrices R(k), P(k) and P(k/k-1) are all assumed to be nonsingular.

In practice a modified Fadeev algorithm, where the matrix A is changed to triangular form prior to annulment of C, is more suitable for systolic array processing. This is summarised as

$$\begin{bmatrix} A & B \\ -C & D \end{bmatrix} \longrightarrow \begin{bmatrix} TA & TB \\ -C & D \end{bmatrix} \longrightarrow \begin{bmatrix} TA & TB \\ 0 & D+CA^{-1}B \end{bmatrix} \qquad (12.13)$$

where TA is an upper triangular matrix.

Pass	A	B	C	D	Result
1	I	$\hat{\underline{x}}(k-1/k-1)$	$-F(k-1)$	0	$\hat{\underline{x}}(k/k-1)$
2	$P^{-1}(k-1/k-1)$	$F^T(k-1)$	$-F(k-1)$	$Q(k-1)$	$P(k/k-1)$
3	$R(k)$	I	$-H^T(k)$	0	$H^T(k)R^{-1}(k)$
4	$P(k/k-1)$	I	$-I$	0	$P^{-1}(k/k-1)$
5	I	$H(k)$	$-H^T(k)R^{-1}(k)$	$P^{-1}(k/k-1)$	$P^{-1}(k/k)$
6	$P^{-1}(k/k)$	$H^T(k)R^{-1}(k)$	I	0	$K(k)$
7	I	$\hat{\underline{x}}(k/k-1)$	$H(k)$	$\underline{z}(k)$	$\tilde{\underline{z}}(k)$
8	I	$\tilde{\underline{z}}(k)$	$-K(k)$	$\hat{\underline{x}}(k/k-1)$	$\hat{\underline{x}}(k/k)$

**Table 12.1 Data and results from application of Fadeev algorithm to
Kalman filter equations**

12.4 SYSTOLIC ARCHITECTURE

The architecture for performing the computation outlined in the last section
is based on LU decomposition. Fig.12.4 contains a schematic diagram of the array for
the case where n = 4. Each pass is a two-step operation involving triangularisation of
A following by transforming C into a null matrix (equation (12.13)). This was achieved
in Reference 1 by defining separate computing modes for both the internal and the
boundary cells. Thus the data for A and B would be fed through the array first in the
triangularisation mode. With this step completed, the array would then accept the
elements of the C and D matrices and nullify C, using diagonal elements of the upper
triangular matrix A stored in local memory as pivots.

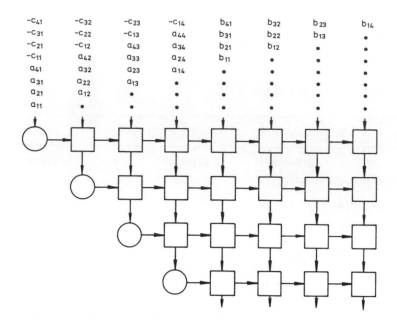

Fig.12.4 Systolic array for parallel Kalman filtering based on the Fadeev algorithm and QR decomposition (n = 4)

On examining the array more closely it was found that a continuous input of data could be achieved whereby it was possible to enter the elements of C and D without having to wait until the triangularisation mode was completed. In addition, it was noted that by a minor modification, the internal cells need only have one mode. The boundary cells now operate in a cyclostatic fashion changing from one calculation mode to the other after a fixed number of timesteps, with the triangularisation mode, for example, rippling through the array as described later. To achieve this the cell operations are now defined as follows.

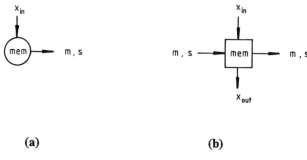

(a)   (b)

Fig.12.5 (a) Boundary cell; (b) Internal cell

Boundary cell (Fig.12.5a):

Mode 1 for triangularisation of A.

If $x_{in} = 0$, $m = 0, s = 0$

If $x_{in} > mem$, $m = mem/x_{in}$, $s = 1$, $mem = x_{in}$

If $x_{in} < mem$, $m = x_{in}/mem$, $s = 0$

Mode 2 for nullifying C.

$m = x_{in}/mem$, $s = 0$

Internal cell (Fig.12.5b):

If $s = 1$, $x_{out} = mem - m.x_{in}$, $mem = x_{in}$

If $s = 0$, $x_{out} = x_{in} - m.mem$

The boundary cell finds the pivot between nearest neighbours and calculates the multiplying factor m. The internal cell handles the rest of the calculation involved in multiplying the elements of one row of a matrix by m and subtracting them from corresponding elements in succeeding rows, as needed for elimination. The variable mem is data stored in local memory of a cell and s represents a control variable.

12.5 OCCAM SIMULATION

The operation of the architecture for parallel Kalman filtering has been simulated on a VAX 8650 computer using Occam 1. Occam proved to be particularly suited for this work as it describes the network of processors using channels and arrays of channels. However it will only handle one-dimensional arrays which made simulation of two-dimensional arrays more complicated but this language limitation has been removed in Occam 2.

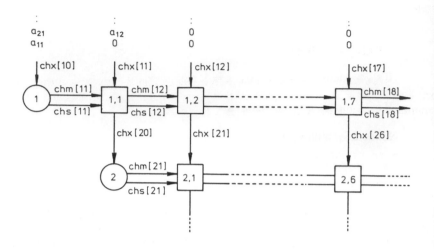

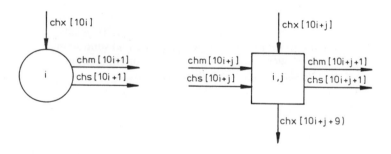

Fig.12.6 Labelling and numbering of channels for the occam simulation of the array in Fig.12.4

The code was set up in the following manner. First a detailed diagram was drawn with all the channels named and numbered. A section of this is shown in Fig.12.6. The method of numbering employed allows the simulated array to be two-dimensional even though the arrays of channels are one-dimensional. Each internal cell is numbered (i,j), where i is the row number and j is the column number. All the channels going into the cell are numbered $(10i+j)$. The boundary cells are treated in a similar fashion, although since there is only one per row they only need an i value. In this case all channels going in are numbered $(10i)$.

A section of code describing the operation of the boundary cells and a separate section for the internal cells was then written (Appendix) and the whole array simulated simply by using PAR statements. Notice that for the internal cell the PAR statements are

PAR i = (1 FOR 4)
   PAR j = (1 FOR 7)

even though in practice 7 cells are only needed for the first row of the systolic array when n = 4. The reason is that in a parallel statement i has 4 values simultaneously and therefore

PAR j = (1 FOR (8-i))
is not acceptable.

Systolic array cells have local memory, but in an Occam simulation the cells only perform operations and cannot store data from one timestep to the next. Therefore, there has to be a global memory handler: at each timestep the data in cell memory is passed to the memory handler which returns it to the same cell at the beginning of the next timestep. The code in the Appendix describes the memory handling of the entire array.

The final step was to connect the input and output channels to the data and a results file respectively. All the channels at the end of a row of the simulated array were output to ANY, effectively to forget the data. A channel cannot take in a new value before it has output the previous ones to somewhere else. If the output is not required an ANY statement will collect the data and forget it.

The actual architecture was designed for real numbers and therefore the libraries IOPROCS.OCC, FILEHDR.OCC and FLOAT32.OCC were used. This allowed real numbers to be read in and out of the simulated array from external files and for single length arithmetic operations to be carried out on these numbers. Within the section of code for the boundary cell the subroutine RealOp (mout, xin, Div, mxin) is called which performs the operation mout = xin/mxin. Every time the program was compiled, then subroutine libraries were attached and the implementation limit quickly reached. By changing the default value of the usage-check in the compiler from TRUE to FALSE it proved possible to compile much larger programs.

12.6 ARCHITECTURE OPERATION

The Occam simulation of the parallel Kalman filter architecture outlined in Section 12.5 facilitated a detailed examination of its operation. This section discusses the performance in terms of speedup and processor utilisation and indicates two ways in which these may be improved.

The necessity of switching the operation of the complete array during each pass, as required in Reference 1, can be avoided. Thus, the boundary cells change mode every n timesteps but not all at the same instant. The change of the second boundary cell occurs two timesteps after the first and so on down the array. Also the memory for all processing cells in the array is reset to zero at intervals of 2n timesteps. Again this is staggered in time. This improvement now allows the array to process continuous streams of data but will not offer significant improvement in speedup without proper scheduling of the passes. The reason is that most of the eight passes require results from a previous one. The array is best utilised by scheduling the passes as in Table 12.2. Here passes 1, 2 and 3 are performed continuously as are passes 7 and 5.

Passes	Processing times
1, 2, 3	$9n-1$
4	$5n-1$
7, 5	$7n-1$
6	$5n-1$
8	$5n-1$

Table 12.2 Scheduling of passes and processing times for the parallel Kalman filter architecture

Table 12.2 also contains the number of timesteps for the data to actually pass through the array. The significant amount of time required for data manipulation is not included. The total time for the eight passes is now $(31n-5)$ compared with one in excess of $(40n-8)$ for the Yeh architecture. This constitutes a computing speedup of up to 129%.

Another strategy for improving speedup is to use a separate systolic array for each pass. This has the added advantage that the array size can be adjusted to improve processor utilisation for each pass, although, the overall processor utilisation will fall. The single array must be able to handle matrices up to order n and therefore in pass seven for example, where the vectors $x(k/k-1)$ and $z(k)$ are involved, the majority of cells are not used. Fig.12.7 illustrates how these arrays can be organised and Table 12.3 shows the array sizes required together with timing information which allows the data flows between the arrays to be scheduled efficiently.

For example consider the loop containing the measurement update equation, with passes 1, 7 and 8, shown in Fig.12.7. The information from array 1 starts to emerge after 3n timesteps and this is passed straight into array 7. However, because pass 7 has the identity matrix in position A of equation (12.9), it can start n timesteps before this i.e. 2n timesteps after array 1 has started. After a further 3n timesteps the result from array 7 starts to appear but again array 8 can be started m timesteps before this i.e. (5n-m) timesteps after array 1 has started. Similarly the result of pass 8 starts to emerge after a further 3m timesteps but again array 1 can start n timesteps before the data from array 8 arrives at it. Therefore array 1 can start again (3m-n) timesteps after array 8 has started. The iteration time for the state update part of Fig.12.7 is then calculated as (4n + 2m) timesteps. This analysis has been applied to produce the complete data flow schedule of Fig.12.8 which contains

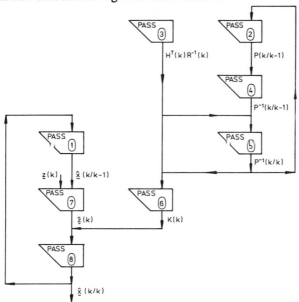

Fig.12.7 Data flows for parallel Kalman filter with a separate systolic array for each pass

timings for all eight arrays. The iteration period was calculated as 6n + m timesteps, a great improvement on that of (31n-5) timesteps which was obtained using only one array. The use of a separate array for each pass can therefore produce speedup of up to 516% as compared to a single array and multiple passes. There is an even greater improvement on the sequential processing time, of order n^2.

Not only is this combination of arrays fast but it uses the processing cells relatively efficiently. The processor efficiency of the matrix times vector array described previously is 50%, i.e. these processing cells are used almost 50% of the time. For this architecture the efficiency is around 28% which for a combination of systolic arrays is very good.

Feature Pass	1	2	3	4	5	6	7
Array size n_1	n	n	m	n	m	n	n
$n_1 \diagdown n_2$ n_2	1	n	m	m	n	m	1
Timesteps for one pass	4n	5n-1	4m+n-1	5n-1	3m+2n-1	4n+m-1	3n+m
Timesteps for which a cell is used in a pass	2n	2n	m+n	2n	m+n	2n	n+m
Timesteps before first data out	3n	3n	3m	3n	3m	3n	3n
Timesteps ahead an array can start	n	0	–	0	2m	0	n

Table 12.3 Array sizes and timing information for parallel Kalman filter implementation in Fig.12.7

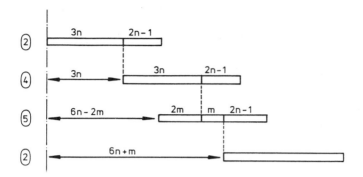

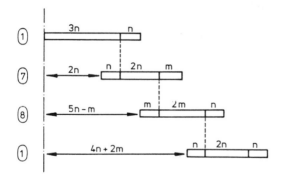

Fig.12.8 Data flow schedule for the implementation in Fig.12.7

12.7 CONCLUSIONS

Occam simulation has been used to study an architecture for parallel Kalman filtering recently proposed in the literature. This is based on a systolic array implementation of the Fadeev algorithm. It has been concluded that

(a)   The need for the internal cells to have two modes of operation can be avoided with a minor modification.

(b) The array can operate in a cyclostatic mode with continuous streams of data. Correct scheduling of the eight passes will then produce a speedup of better than 11%.

(c) The use of a separate array for each pass, coupled with a planned data flow schedule, offers further speedup of up to 516% coupled with good efficiency of usage of the processing cells of around 28%.

(d) Both implementations give a speedup of $0(n^2)$ compared with a single processor implementation .

REFERENCES

1. Yeh, H.G., 1986, "Kalman filtering and systolic processors", Proc. Int. Conf. on Acoustics, Speech and Signal Processing, Tokyo, pp.2139-2142.

2. Kung, H.T. and Leiserson, C.,1978, "Algorithms for VLSI processor arrays", Carnegie-Mellon University, Dept. of Computer Science, Report No. CMU-C5-79-103.

3. McCanny, J.V. and McWhirter, J.G., 1987, "Some systolic array developments in the United Kingdom", Computer, Vol. 20, No. 7, pp.51-63.

4. Fadeev, D.K. and Fadeeva, V.N., 1963, "Computational methods of linear algebra", W.H. Freeman and Co., pp.150.

APPENDIX

Occam Coding for the Boundary Cell, Internal Cell and Memory Handler (n = 4)

1. Boundary Cell

```
PAR i = [1 FOR 4]
   VAR c,n,z,xin,mout,sout,sqm,sqx,res,mxim,mxout:
   SEQ
      PAR
         chx[i*10]? xin
         chmemi[i]? mxin
         chm[(i*10)+1]! mout
         chs[(i*10)+1]! sout
      c:= k\8
      n:= 2*i
      IF
         (c=((n 1)\8)) OR (c=(n\8)) OR (c=((n+1)\8)) OR
         (c=((n+2)\8))
            SEQ
               RealOp(sqm,mxin,Mul,mxin)
               RealOp(sqx,xin,Mul,xin)
               RealCompare(res,sqx,sqm)
               IF
                  (xin = 0) AND (mxin = 0)
                     SEQ
                        mout:= 0
                        sout:= 0
                        mxout:= mxin
                  (res = 1)
                     SEQ
                        sout:= 1
                        RealOp(mout,mxin,Div,xin)
                        mxout:=xin
                  TRUE
                     SEQ
                        sout:= 0
                        RealOp(mout,xin,Div,mxin)
                        mxout:= mxin
         TRUE
            SEQ
               IF
                  mxin=0
                     mout:= 0
                  mxin<>0
                     RealOp(mout,xin,Div,mxin)
               mxout:= mxin
               sout:= 0
      PAR
         chmemo[i]! mxout
```

2. Internal Cell

```
PAR i = [1 FOR 4]
  PAR j = [1 FOR 7]
    VAR z,xout,mout,sout,xin,min,sin,mxin,mxout:
    SEQ
      PAR
        chx[(10*i)+j]? xin
        chm[(10*i)+j]? min
        chs[(10*i)+j]? sin
        chmemi[(10*i)+j]? mxin
        chx[(10*i)+(j+9)]! xout
        chm[(10*i)+(j+1)]! mout
        chm[(10*i)+(j+1)]! sout
      IF
        sin = 1
          SEQ
            RealOp(z,min,Mul,xin)
            RealOp(xout,mxin,Sub,z)
            mxout:= xin
        sin = 0
          SEQ
            RealOp(z,min,Mul,mxin)
            RealOp(xout,xin,Sub,z)
            mxout:= mxin
      mout:= min
      sout:= sin
      PAR
        chmemo[(10*i)+j]! mxout
```

3. Memory handling

```
SEQ
  IF
    k = 0
      -- initialise memory to zero
      PAR i = [1 FOR 4]
        PAR
          chmemi[i]! 0
          PAR j = [1 FOR 7]
            chmemi[(10*i)+j]! 0
    TRUE
      -- input memory
      PAR i = [1 FOR 4]
        PAR
          chmemi[i]!m[i]
          PAR j = [1 FOR 7]
            chmemi[(10*i)+j]! m[(10*i)+j]
      -- output memory
      PAR i = [1 FOR 4]
        PAR
          chmemo[i]? m[i]
          PAR j = [1 FOR 7]
            chmemo[(10*i)+j]? m[(10*i)+j]
```

Chapter 13

PACE: a VLSI architecture

Dr. Simon Jones

13.1 INTRODUCTION

The objective of this Chapter is to introduce PACE (Programmable Adaptive Computing Engine) objectives, implementation, design issues and applications together with an overview of the embryonic PACE research program.

13.2 PACE RESEARCH OBJECTIVES

The PACE research objectives can be summarised as the search for a flexible programmable parallel architecture suitable for the support of control/robotics applications which

(a) Provides efficient parallel processing support for a wide range of computational tasks.

(b) Allows a flexible set of tradeoffs between processor allocation and computation speed to be made.

(c) Meets the technological constraints of current and future VLSI processes.

(d) Supports fault-tolerance and graceful degradation for high-reliability applications.

13.3 PACE CONCEPT

The PACE concept is that of a regular array of largely identical pace processing elements (PPEs) of programmable functionality and programmable interconnect topology.

PACE comprises 3 distinct classes of cell, namely

(a) PPE cells that comprise the processing elements of the chip.

(b) Edge cells to connect off-chip to other PACE chips or to peripheral devices.

(c) Communication cells to connect PPE and Edge cells in the appropriate configuration.

The desired processor is realised by: programming the appropriate function in the PPEs and edge cells, and configuring the communication cells to create the desired signal paths.

13.4 PACE OPERATION

PACE can operate in 3 different modes: Irregular, Regular and Mixed.

13.4.1 PACE Irregular Mode

This mode is characterised by a large number of PPEs being programmed with dissimilar functions and the connectivity cells realising a topologically complex structure. This mode is used to implement many of the computational tasks, whose structure does not naturally simplify into simple scalar-vector or vector-vector operations.

Fig.13.1 gives an example of a PACE array in irregular mode, configured to execute a simple function.

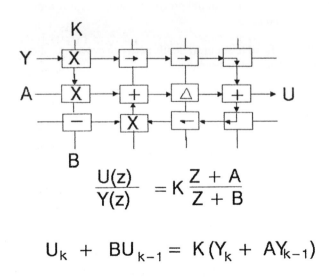

$$\frac{U(z)}{Y(z)} = K\frac{Z + A}{Z + B}$$

$$U_k + BU_{k-1} = K(Y_k + AY_{k-1})$$

Fig.13.1 PACE irregular mode

13.4.2 PACE Regular Mode

This mode is characterised by a large number of PEs being programmed with the same function and the connectivity cells realising a regular (eg. linear, 2-D array, triangular) topology. Here PACE operates in a manner akin to a systolic array, but with greater programmability and connectivity.

Fig.13.2 gives an example of a PACE array in regular mode. configured to execute a simple digital filter.

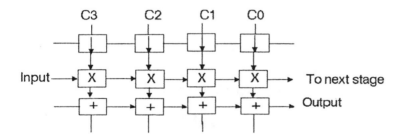

4 – stage transversal filter (Version 1)

Fig.13.2 PACE regular mode

13.4.3 PACE Mixed Mode

The programmability and configurability of the PACE structure allows it to use a mixture of both irregular and irregular formats. For example, the regular mode could be used for the bulk of the computation and be surrounded with irregular PACE structures to make decisions and/or format data for correct input or output to the system.

13.4.4 PACE Operational Tradeoffs

The programmable functionality allows PACE to be configured to satisfy a range of user and resource-directed tradeoffs. For example, Fig.13.3 shows the PACE filter in Fig.13.2, reorganised to trade off performance for a reduced number of PPEs. Other tradeoffs such as increased connectivity for higher PPE utilisation are also possible.

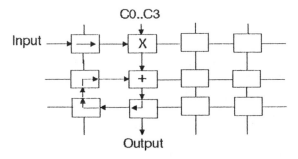

4 – stage transversal filter (Version 2)

Fig.13.3 Alternative PACE arrangement

13.5 PACE ADVANTAGES

Such an architecture as PACE confers many advantages for the implementation of computational structures including,

(a) Natural design: the PACE structure maps closely to the control-flow design methodology of the design engineer, offering potential simplifications of design coding, testing and implementation.

(b) Lower costs: the simple structure of the PPEs means that many PPEs can be integrated on a single silicon chip thus reducing system costs. Furthermore, the flexibility and wide range of applications, means that PACE design costs can be amortised over many different systems.

(c) Wide applicability: a few PACE chips, by suitable programming can support a wide range of applications for little extra cost.

(d) High-speed: as PACE functions are embedded in hardware, they operate significantly faster than software emulations of similar functions.

(e) Extendability: more complex functions can be embedded by adding more PPEs to the array. Furthermore, as has been shown it is possible to tradeoff PPEs for increased performance in many cases.

(f) Suitability for VLSI: PACE chips comprise small simple regular structures, with local and hence high-speed communications. Furthermore, only edge cells require pinning-out, reducing pin count. This is especially important with future processes, as PACE pin-out rises only very slowly (as the square root of the number of cells) with more PPEs being integrated on a chip.

All these factors are widely accepted as being characteristic of an architecture well suited to VLSI implementation.

13.6 PACE IMPLEMENTATION

13.6.1 Configuration

As previously stated, the desired PACE architecture is realised by setting the functionality and configuration of the PPEs appropriately. This configuration can be achieved in one of 3 distinct ways:-

(a) Static configuration: here the processor structure is defined at fabrication time by a programmable mask (cf. ROM chips) or on-site by blowing 'once-only' fuses or programming non-volatile storage (eg. EPROMs).

(b) Pseudo-static: here the chips configured at system set-up time, this allows maximum flexibility as the same PACE chips could be used for a wide range of functions but requires extra system-level logic to store the configuration patterns and set them up.

(c) Dynamic: here the PACE array is not only set-up initially, but changes its structure in real-time on the basis of external control and internal status information. This option may require more sophisticated PPE and system logic, but confers the ability to alter the processor to match the changing structure of the computation.

13.6.2 Layering

At the heart of the PACE implementation are the 3 layers of the PACE processor

(a) Processing layer this comprises all the PPEs. PPEs execute their programmed function every clock cycle (or multiple of clock cycles). Typical functions would include add, move AND, OR etc. Multiply need not be a primitive PPE operation as it could be constructed out of several add and store PPEs. The particular set of functions that a PPE can execute can only be determined by a complex set of tradeoffs between applications requirement and silicon overheads and is one of the key tasks in the PACE research program. The data for PPE functions is presented either from communication cells connected to the PPE or from store, local to the PPE.

(b) Communications layer: this layer is responsible for implementing the desired topology on the PACE array and for transferring signals between PPEs. The communications cells are connected both 'across' to each other and 'downwards' to the PPEs that they serve.

(c) Loading Layer: this layer is responsible for input of programming data to select PPE functionality and communication cells connectivity. The loading layer connects to both communication cells and PPEs. For static PACE chips, no programming layers are needed as the functionality and connectivity are determined at fabrication.

13.6.3 Implementation Tradeoffs

This section outlines some of the implementation tradeoffs in the processing, communication and loading layers that need to be addressed in the PACE research program.

(a) Processing layer: A more complex PPE will increase functionality, but reduce the number of PPEs that can be fitted onto a chip and increase system cost.

(b) Communication layer: The more richly interconnected the communication layer, the more sophisticated the interconnect network that can be realised. Furthermore, the more communication pathways exist, the greater the number of PPEs that can be utilised. However, communication cells occupy silicon area and more communication cells means fewer PPEs. Nonetheless, the fact that the PPE is likely to be considerably larger than the communication cell does argue for a richly connected communications layer to optimise PPE utilisation.

(c) Loading layer: As previously stated, statically configured PACE arrays do not have a loading layer. For pseudo-static PACE devices, where loading is performed relatively infrequently, one can use place PACE into loading mode (via an external signal) and use a serial 'scan-path' (shift register) to load in PPE function and connectivity information (possibly utilising the communications layer). In this case, then, loading is unlikely to be a major silicon overhead.

It is with dynamic loading (viz. where the PACE array adaptively restructures itself) that the issues become less clear. Protocols need to be devised such that rapid and reliable state changes can be achieved.

13.7 PACE PROGRAMMING

As previously stated, PACE maps well with the control- flow design methodology and is relatively easy to configure in static and pseudo-static modes. Furthermore, it is not unreasonable to assume that the design of CAD suites which take in a high-level description of the system to be realised and the optimisation criteria to produce a configuration for a PACE array, together with performance data could be engineered.

13.8 PACE FAULT-TOLERANCE

As previously, stated one of the objectives of the PACE program was to support fault-tolerance for high-reliability systems. Three main classes of fault-tolerant operation can be supported.

(a) Minor failure: The programmable array and interconnect is well suited to these tasks, as failing cells can be configured around and spare PPEs incorporated.

(b) Medium failure: In the event of more failures than spares, the use of performance/PPE tradeoffs, as discussed above, could also be used to maintain system uptime, albeit at the cost of degraded performance.

(c) Major failure: In the event of major failures, the PACE array could be configured to keep critical functions performing even if other system elements were lost.

13.9 PACE RESEARCH PROGRAM

This section discusses the research program at UCNW about to commence into the design and evaluation of PACE structures.

The PACE research program has just received SERC funding for equipment, materials and manpower. The objectives of this research are,

(a) To investigate the design constraints and cost- effective constructs for the PACE array using the areas of real-time control and robotics as the applications environment. This is to be achieved through the development of an executable Transputer-based OCCAM simulator/specification of the PACE structure. OCCAM and the Transputer have been selected because of the ability of OCCAM to express parallel constructs and for Transputer arrays to model the PPEs.

(b) Design and construction of a gate-array model of a PACE PPE based on the information gained from the simulator and the construction of a small PACE array for design and concept verification.

(c) Comparison of the PACE concept with Transputer arrays and a fine-grain array processor (GAPP) for particular control algorithms.

From this research a clear understanding of the design issues involved in the construction and application of PACE structures can be gained.

This research can be used as a springboard to lead on to the implementation of a full-custom VLSI PACE chips around which CAD suites and demonstrator applications can be constructed. Future work is also planned into applying and enhancing the fault-tolerance faculties of PACE and expanding the application areas considered.

13.10 CONCLUSIONS

This Chapter has reviewed the objectives, design, implementation and applications of PACE. It has been argued that PACE offers several significant advantages for realising cost-effective high-performance systems.

ACKNOWLEDGEMENTS

The author would like to thank Drs P.J. Fleming and D.I. Jones, for the many long and fruitful discussions which have led to the conception and development of PACE.

Index